The 1-2-2 Jug Offense for Attacking Basketball's Zones

The 1-2-2 Jug Offense
for Attacking
Basketball's Zones

Art Poulin

Parker Publishing Company, Inc.
West Nyack, New York

Library of Congress Cataloging in Publication Data

Poulin, Art
    The 1-2-2 jug offense for attacking basketball's
zones.

        Includes index.
        1. Basketball—Offense.   2. Basketball—Coaching.
I. Title.   II. Title: The one-two-two jug offense for
attacking basketball's zones.
GV889.P68   1983   796.32'32   83-8180
ISBN 0-13-635466-1

This book is dedicated to the many coaches who have helped me in learning more about the great game of basketball and, in particular, to Mike Hayes and Mario Balestrieri, co-coaches, whose work with the Jug helped to make it such a success.

WHY JUG?

Today's coaches must have their teams ready to attack any of the sophisticated zone defenses now in use. The 1-2-2 Jug, an all-purpose offense that has evolved over years of work, is a simple, yet sure-fire way of beating *all* zones; and within it are many features that may be used against man-for-man defense. The Jug is a combination of several effective attacks blended into one basic offense.

Employing the Jug as the sole offense solves two large problems faced by coaches: preparing for any zone defense that might be encountered during the course of a season and preparing for those defenses without having to sacrifice valuable time needed for coaching all other aspects of the game. Within the Jug attack are most of the essentials found in most zone offenses: ball movement and player movement to beat the zone's shifts, splitting the seams in the zone, cutting through and behind the lines of defense, overloading the court to outnumber the defense, and working on the specific weaknesses within each different type of zone defense. The Jug concept uses several options from its basic set in such a manner that weaknesses inherent in each zone and shortcomings of individual opponents are exploited. Adjustments in the Jug may be made to overcome an opponent's strengths and to utilize the strong points of the Jugging team. By using the Jug, your team can smash the orthodox zones and the special combination zones. Without making major modifications, you can use the Jug attack advantageously for the special-situation shot, against traps, and as a basis for auxiliary plays and the secondary phase of your fast break.

Players like the Jug. It allows all of them to handle the ball and score. Everyone on a Jugging team is active in the offense, and everyone may have the opportunity to break free with and without the ball. Players develop confidence when they have a workable offense that has a pattern—a continuity—that is easily understood, produces positive results, and is versatile. The medium-range shooter will find natural spots in the Jug. Because a large part of the Jug is inside oriented, the strong low post and rebounder types get many scoring opportunities.

Even teams that meet only a few zones in a season can profit by using the Jug as their sole zone offense. The basic Jug movement can be learned in a relatively short time. The expansion of the offense by adding options is explained in this book; however, it is not necessary to use many of them to run a successful Jug offense. You will find that as you become more familiar with the Jug you will be able to create options of your own. Those you choose to use from this book, and your original options, will benefit your team immensely if it meets a preponderance of zones.

This book presents the Jug in such a manner that you may duplicate the progression from chapter to chapter as you teach it to your team. As the team masters the initial action, other phases may be added. Certain options have been found to be more successful against certain defenses, against specific types of opponents, and at particular points in a game. It is not necessary to use all the options presented in order to win with the Jug. You can select that part of the Jug that fits your needs, your team, your philosophy; you will add wrinkles of your own to make the Jug your own zone offense.

I have made no attempt to cover in detail the individual offensive fundamentals used by Jugging players. The skills inherent in basketball are the skills needed for winning with the Jug. The Jug is no cure-all for sloppy ball handling, faulty footwork, weak rebounding, and poor shot selection.

The chapter on drills includes methods used for general offensive work, with particular emphasis on skills used in the Jug. You may wish to include these and/or use your own special drills, modified to highlight Jugging skills.

An apology is in order for some of the attempts at humor here. It is essential for practical reasons to give names to certain aspects and parts of the game of basketball. By trying to attach some humor or some distinctive name to some of these, I have attempted to make it easier for players to remember them. Thus when the basic Jug formation is expanded against the half-court trap, it is called "Carboy." I bring a 5-gallon carboy out on the practice court and compare it to the gallon jug used when this phase of the offense is first introduced to the team. I want the players to grasp the concept of playing in an expanded 1-2-2 formation. When an option in the Carboy action was developed, it seemed natural to call it "Cargirl." Corny? Definitely! I hope that it helps my players remember the term and its meaning in our offense.

One last apology. Use of the masculine pronouns and male-oriented words in this book is due to habit and a desire to not use the clumsy "he/she" form throughout. No slur toward the other sex is intended. I have also seen high school girls' teams use the Jug very effectively. As with most aspects of the great game of basketball, the Jug is suited for both sexes.

Art Poulin

CONTENTS

Chapter 3

Expanding the Jug

Chapter 4

Stick a Flower in the Jug

Chapter 8

Auxiliary Jug Play   **125**

Chapter 9

Jugging in Game Situations   **153**

Chapter 10

Jug Drills   **167**

Index   **191**

The 1-2-2 Jug Offense for Attacking Basketball's Zones

1

THE JUG CONCEPT AND PLAYER PLACEMENT

INITIAL SET

"Jug" refers to the initial 1-2-2 set for this zone offense (Figure 1-1). The descriptive term was borrowed from the famed former coach of Long Island University, Clair Bee, whose 1-2-2 zone *defense* was so named.

In the Jug *offense*, the ball-handling point guard is the Cork (1 in Figure 1-1). The two wing men in the next line are pinched in at the ends of the free throw line to form the Shoulders (2, 3) of the Jug. The bottom of the Jug is formed by the two Baseliners (4, 5), who are located at the free throw lane bricks. These positions are merely starting spots. Players move during the pattern of play, and frequently their movement starts prior to the entry of the ball into the Jug action.

A brief description of the preliminary action in the offense is included here to cover the skills and attributes generally needed by players using the Jug. In Chapter 2, the moves of each player will be discussed in detail.

The usual key to the start of the offense is the first pass, which is normally from Cork to Shoulder. At times

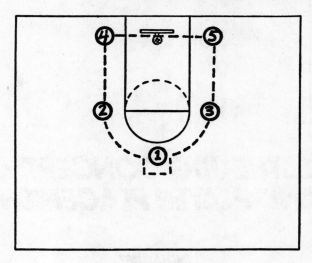

Figure 1-1

this is an easy pass, but it is often made difficult by hustling aggressive defenders. Ideally the Shoulder obtains the ball at his basic Jug spot, but this is frequently impossible. He may be forced to move up and out to open a passing lane. Likewise, the Cork may have to dribble to one side to get his pass off to the Shoulder. The Shoulder may even have to come far out to act as a release man for the Cork, who has picked up his dribble.

Once the ball is at the Shoulder (Figure 1-2), the offense is on. The Baseliner on the ball side blocks the nearest defensive low man as the other Baseliner comes across the lane around the block to receive the ball from the Shoulder. Meanwhile the other Shoulder (without the ball) has dropped in to rebound the potential shot by the Baseliner (Figure 1-2).

For a general picture of the continuity, assume that no shot develops and the ball is passed on the periphery back out to the Cork. He now swings the ball to the weak side for a different type of offensive move in the reverse action. If no shot is taken here, the ball is again

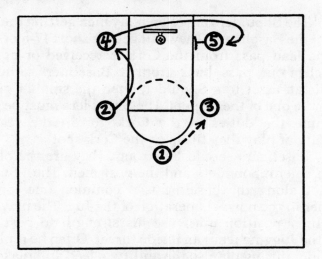

Figure 1-2

brought back to the side initially attacked, forcing continuous defensive adjustments. Throughout all of this movement the Baseliners and Shoulders become quite involved
in rebounding responsibilities.

FITTING PLAYERS TO SPOTS

The Cork has to be a good ball handler. He starts
the ball action in the offense, and most frequently he
indicates the type of Jug or the Jug option to be used.
Therefore he should have good court savvy, confidence in
himself, and leadership ability. It helps if he is tall, but a
short, active guard type can handle the Cork spot.

The ability to hit the outside shot gives the Cork
extra ammunition against any front-line defenders he
faces. Quickness helps immeasurably in this position. The
Cork must be able to take pressure and should have the
endurance to withstand full-court harassment and still set
up and run the offense.

The Shoulders are often relay men getting the ball to one of the Baseliners. They will get the short 17-foot shot after the lead pass from the Cork is received or after a quick clear-out pass back from a Baseliner. Although height is an asset to a Shoulder, often the smaller guard can handle one of these spots. The Shoulders must be able to assume the duties of the Cork, for in the regular continuity of play they fill in at the Cork spot.

Baseliners should be strong. They are the blockers, the chief rebounders and the post men. The 12-to-15-foot shot along the baseline is a common one for the Baseliner in the normal operation of the Jug. The player at a Baseliner position must use his strength to post low, giving the Jugging team an inside threat. Often he replaces a Shoulder during play, so the ability to feed and make the medium distance jump shot from in front is important.

As with any offense, you must evaluate your personnel carefully to place them in the most advantageous positions. Comparing defensive and offensive strengths of individual players on the team and fitting them together in balance become critical in an offense that capitalizes on individual offensive strengths. If all teams were composed of big, smart, quick, agile, aggressive, dedicated, deadly shooting, accurate-passing, well-coordinated players in every position, any offensive tactic would probably be successful—and coaches would have to look for employment in other fields. However, most teams are not in this position, and it becomes necessary for the coach to adjust personnel with care.

The big, slow starter usually fits into the Jug as a Baseliner. Yet he may be considered for a job at the Shoulder if there are other big players on his team who can handle the Baseliner spot better.

The good rebounder who is a weak shooter may be used most effectively as a Shoulder, where his lack of scoring ability is offset by the many rebounding opportunities obtained from that spot. He'll have to be used as a feeder and screener, too.

Because the Baseliner has the least amount of passing to do, this might be the best place for the weakest ball handler, especially if he has some size. He can use his rebounding ability here and contribute even more if he has the necessary medium-distance shooting ability.

The poor shooter who can handle the ball well may work out as a Cork. His key pass to the Shoulder is the heart of the start of most Jug action. Sacrificing scoring punch at the Cork spot is justified if ball-handling skill is there

If the player chosen to be the Cork is not the most court-wise man on the team, another player can key the offense. He can do this from another position and take some of the pressure off the Cork, who can then concentrate on getting the offense started.

DISADVANTAGES OF JUGGING

Nothing is perfect. There are disadvantages if a coach puts all his basketballs in one basket by running only one offense against all zones. He must recognize the disadvantages and offset them.

If it is known that a team runs the Jug against all zones, many zoning opponents will count on having to defense only one offense. This would give them confidence they might not otherwise have had. To counter this the Jugging team must have enough flexibility and variation within its offense to present continuing problems to the prepared zoners.

The tendency for players to become automatons whenever they have mastered a phase of the Jug presents a challenge to the coach. He must continually work for near perfection in running the simple offense, yet he has to be alert for lack of spantaneity among the players during the repetitive phase of training.

Game slippage, the inevitable lapses by players during a game, is a problem in the Jug as much as it is in other offenses and phases of basketball. Keeping the Jug basic enough and adding necessary options when the team is ready for new material is a judgment problem for the coach in keeping ahead of his opponents.

The team that is extremely limited in its personnel may have difficulty using the Jug. If you do not have a good ball-handling player at the Cork position, much of the bite of the offense will be lost. But ball handlers can be trained. The Jug coach must concern himself with this training and, in planning for the future, make sure that lower-level, younger players will be ready to play at the Cork position when they reach the varsity level.

A basketball team without some effective size is usually hurting. A small Jug team must make up for this lack by aggressive rebounding, placing emphasis on gaining good rebound position, taking good shots, and being patient while running the offense. If there is just one big man available on a team, he may have to be a blocker from his Baseliner position while the other Baseliner does the shooting from along the baseline. The big man becomes the primary post and is given more rebound responsibility.

The versatility of the Jug, the many options available, and the adjustments to combat varieties of zone defenses should outweigh the weaknesses of players on a team.

2

INTRODUCING THE TEAM TO THE JUG

When the Jug is being presented to a team for the first time or is being reintroduced to returning players at the beginning of a season, a chalkboard for diagrams of the initial set and the designation of the player spots is helpful. After a description and illustration of the Jug, the next step is an actual dummy set-up on the half court with players in the five Jug spots. At that point the team should walk through the first phase of the Jug action. Repeat the walk-through, then speed it up until it becomes a run-through, and, finally, add a token zone defense.

THE BASIC JUG ACTION

After stationing players in the starting spots, give the ball to the Cork. He is given only two options: a pass to either one of the two Shoulders. The pass he elects establishes the strong side, which is on the ball side of the court.

The Shoulder, receiving the ball, immediately faces the basket by turning to the outside, pivoting on his outside foot. He passes to the Baseliner *Runner* (4), who has come across from the weak side and around the strong-side Baseliner's block (Figure 1-2).

The Runner receives the ball, squares up to the basket, and shoots. The other Baseliner (5, the *Blocker*) blocks out an inside imaginary opponent. Both Baseliners make their moves just as the Cork passes. This first pass of the Cork designates the Runner (4, the weak-side Base-liner) and the Blocker (5, the strong-side Baseliner).

The weak-side Shoulder (2), who did not receive the Cork's pass, goes down the lane toward the basket as soon as the Cork releases the pass. He watches the ball, which is now at the other Shoulder, and, as he nears the baseline, he establishes himself in a rebounding position on the weak side of the basket (Figure 1-2).

At this point in the first walk-through, when the Runner's shot is taken, you should cover rebounding. By doing it at this particular time in the training process, you put a super emphasis on this important part of the offense.

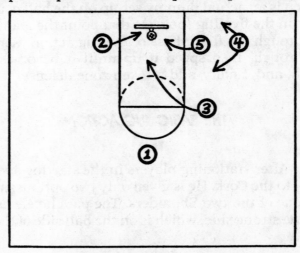

Figure 2-1

The rebound triangle for the shot is made up of the weak-side Shoulder, the feeding Shoulder who moves directly toward the basket from his passing spot, and the Blocker who is on the same side of the basket as the shooter (Figure 2-1).

The shooter must move after he shoots. He becomes practically useless if he stays at the shooting spot. The Runner must be told not to be a spectator after shooting but to move in an arc toward the basket area to help on long rebounds or on defense if the ball is lost. The Cork's primary responsibility is to be a safety on defense. He reacts to the ball. He is ready to get open and shout for the ball if a teammate rebounds the ball and needs to clear it out.

COACHING POINTS

After covering the preliminary movement leading to the Runner's shot, you should present a more extensive session on each player's job and the options that may occur for each player.

Beside his passes to the Shoulders, the Cork has four options:
1. Dribble in order to open passing lanes to the other players.
2. Drive to the basket for a jump shot or dish-off to an open Baseliner or Shoulder.
3. Shoot from outside.
4. Pass directly to a Baseliner who may be open near the basket or along the baseline.

After the Cork passes to a Shoulder, the Cork should seal the pass by stepping toward the receiver. This puts him in a position to help if the ball is mishandled, to play defense if the ball is lost, to get open for a possible outlet return pass, or to keep the defense busy reacting to a possible back cut against an overcommitting defensive man. Even after the Shoulder feeds a Baseliner, the Cork should concern himself with getting free outside for an outlet pass from the Baseliner, who may need help. He may also find a spot on the weak side at which he would be open for a pass across the lane from the Shoulder (Figure 2-2).

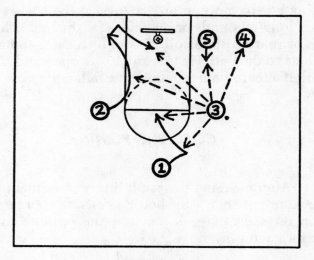

Figure 2-2

Each Shoulder should be active in freeing himself for the pass from the Cork. The Shoulders' movement may even open a driving lane for the Cork. The Shoulders should not feel that it's only up to the Cork to work to get the ball to a Shoulder. The Shoulder should meet the pass from the Cork with elbows out wide and hands up. After receiving the ball, if he is not able to pivot to the outside due to defensive pressure, the Shoulder may pivot to the inside.

Options open to the Shoulder other than the pass to the Runner are (Figure 2-2):

1. Shoot if open and confident in shooting from that spot.
2. Drive to the basket if route is open.
3. Pass to the other Shoulder sliding down the lane.
4. Feed the Blocker who is posting low.
5. If unable to pass to one of the Baseliners, hit the weak-side Shoulder who flashes out from his off-side rebounding spot.
6. Pass to the Cork—either at an outside spot or across the lane if the Cork has found an open spot.

After taking any of his pass options, the Shoulder should move to an open spot for a possible return pass or to the basket to rebound. In the case of the cross-lane pass to the Cork, he may have to take the Cork's position to balance the court. The zone defenders should not be allowed to rest.

The weak-side Shoulder's main job is to get a good rebound position, for the chances are that a shot will go up from the strong side. However, as he moves down the lane he should look for any defensive lapse that might leave him open for a pass from the other Shoulder. If he is open, he should call for the ball and on receiving it go in for a power lay-in. Another option occurs after he gets to a low rebounding spot on the weak side: he may flash to the ball whenever the other Shoulder has it. Frequently this option occurs after the ball is cleared back out to the Shoulder from a Runner who was unable to shoot or feed the Blocker. This is just another example of the need for players to read the defense and react to it.

Each Shoulder must be ready to replace the Cork in driving to the basket. The rule for the Shoulder is to replace the Cork if he drives past the Shoulder on his side of an imaginary line bisecting the court.

While the Cork has the ball, the Baseliners may move to open spots down low, cut across in front of the basket, or signal for a high lob if there is a mismatch in height or an opponent is out of position. The Baseliners should open up the area under the basket if the Cork drives in, and they should be ready for a pass from the driving Cork if the defense collapses on him.

The Baseliner must be ready to move across the lane as the Runner. The faster he goes around the block on the ball side, the better is his chance to get his baseline shot. The Runner normally goes behind the defense to go around the Blocker; however, if the defense plays him strong on the baseline side as he crosses the 3-second area, he may use his Blocker differently and come around him away from the baseline (Figure 2-3).

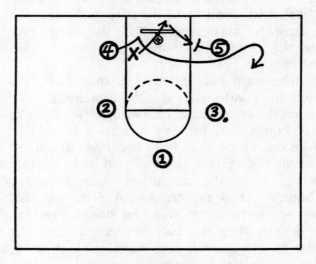

Figure 2-3

The Runner should come closely around the Blocker in order to ensure his anticipated close-in shot. His hands should be up as targets as he comes around the Block. On receiving the ball, he has a shot option as well as a possibility of dumping the ball in to the Blocker posting low. If he dumps the ball, the runner moves for a possible return pass or to aid in the rebounding. A third option is to clear the ball out to the Shoulder or skip-pass out to the Cork.

The Blocker attempts to "chest" the opponent he is screening out as the Runner comes around. As soon as the Runner is past the block, the Blocker pivots to face the ball whether it is in the Runner's possession, or still at the Shoulder. He looks for a pass from either player. The low-post option is still there even after the Runner clears out to the Shoulder. A quick step toward the ball will free the post to receive a pass from the Shoulder.

REBOUNDING RULES

When the team gets to the point where it has the feel of the Jug offense, it is a good idea to designate the following offensive rebounding responsibilities:

The Cork: Looks for the long rebound and is the first man back on defense if the ball is lost; acts as safety valve, looking for outlet passes from teammates who capture rebounds; and, at times, is used as a break-stopper.

The Shoulders: Rebound all shots taken unless given a special assignment, such as break-stopper. The individual coach's rebounding philosophy will dictate whether the Shoulder always follows his own shot.

The Baseliners: Rebound all shots and work at getting the best position to help on rebounding when at the Runner's spot.

The importance of the offensive rebounding part of the Jug can be stressed by running the offense against dummy defense, and stopping play when a shot is taken. Then, check offensive rebounding assignments and the positions taken by each player. Jug players must know the assignments for all spots because of the interchangeable aspects of the offense.

REVERSE ACTION: PICK-ROLL

The reverse action after the first movements on the strong side in the basic Jug attack may be done in two ways: (1) with a pick-and-roll action on the weak side followed by a run around a double block; and (2) with a pass to a V-cutting low man coming out on the weak side, which results in an overload, and a continuation of the basic Jug movement.

The Pick-Roll movement starts as soon as the ball is returned to the Cork after the strong side has been established and probed with the blocking and running action on the baseline (Figure 2-4). When the ball is kicked back out to the Cork after the Runner has gained his place near the baseline, the weak-side Shoulder comes up the lane from his low position with the intent of picking (screening) for the Cork. The Cork, with the ball, starts a drive slanted toward the oncoming Shoulder. Speed is essential here, in order to catch the defense before it shifts back to the ball side.

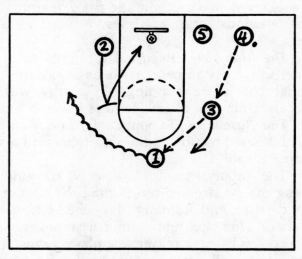

Figure 2-4

Often the Cork and Shoulder can play some two-on-two basketball with the defenders on their side of the court before the rest of the zone reacts to the ball movement. Normal Pick-Roll options are present. The Cork may take a jump shot over the screen if his man is taken out, or he may be able to continue his drive in for a closer shot. If the back defender steps out to stop the Cork's drive, the picker (2), who rolls in, may be open for a pass. This usually produces a lay-in. If the Roller (2) is stopped by a low defender coming across from the other side of the lane (X5 in Figure 2-5), he looks for the option of dropping a pass to the Blocker (5), who has flashed in front of the basket, or to the Runner (4) on the off-side.

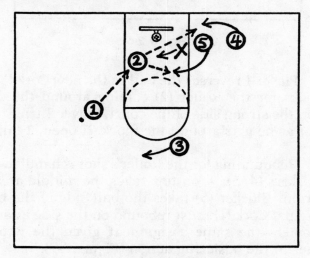

Figure 2-5

During the Pick-Roll movement, the strong-side Shoulder takes the Cork spot and assumes the duties of that position. If the driving Cork doesn't get a shot or doesn't pass off to the Roller, the Blocker (5) maintains his spot down low, and the Runner (4) joins him at his side to form a double block for the Roller (2) coming around them (Figure 2-6).

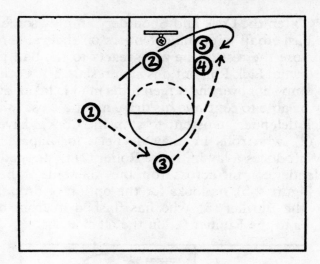

Figure 2-6

Player 1 reverses the ball to the new Cork (3), who then looks for the Roller (2) coming around the double block on the strong side of the court. Player 3 tries to pass to 2 just as he gets around the block. If open, 2 takes the shot.

Rebounding for the Roller's shot is handled by the two blockers (4, 5); 4, on top, takes the middle area, and the bottom Blocker (5) takes the ball side of the basket. The original Cork (1) must rebound on the side away from the shooter—the same assignment given the weak-side Shoulder in the basic Jug action (Figure 2-7).

If rebounding strength is going to be weakened greatly because the original Cork is small or a poor rebounder, an adjustment may be made. After the new Cork (3) passes to the Roller, he interchanges with the original Cork. This reshuffles the better rebounder to the off-side rebounding spot. To be effective, this interchange must be done at top speed.

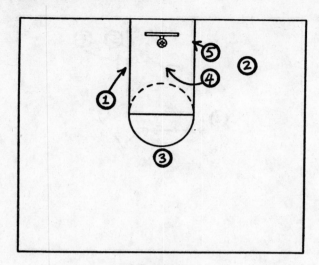

Figure 2-7

OPTIONS IN THE PICK-ROLL

During the beginning of the Pick-Roll on the weak side, and even at the moment of the pick, the Cork can often pass high across to the Runner for his shot. It is important for the Runner to delay his stepping in to form the double block until this pass option is no longer open.

Another pass option for the Cork after the Pick-Roll is one to the strong side Shoulder (3), who is on his way up to replace the Cork (Figure 2-8). If the outside man or men in the zone overplay the potential clear-out pass to the new Cork (3) coming out to the top of the key, 3 steps into the opening that develops at the area just above the free throw line behind the defender(s).

After the Pick-Roll with no shot by either the driving Cork (1) or the Roller (2) and with the ball cleared

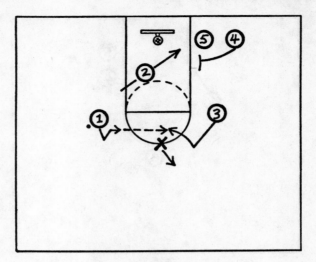

Figure 2-8

out to the new Cork (3), a return pass to the original Cork (1) may produce a shot. This becomes particularly effective after the defense becomes used to the reverse action and overshifts to the strong side when 3 fakes a pass to the strong side and follows this by a right-now pass to 1. As shown in Figure 2-9, a variety of options for 1 occur at this point:

1. Shoot, if open and confident.
2. Drive, if the one-on-one situation is there.
3. Feed the top man of the double block (4), who moves across in front of the basket. While double-blocking with 5, 4 waits for 1 to shoot or drive before making his move; then he goes if there is daylight in front of the basket or on the low weak side. He tries to get the defensive man near him in the block area on his hip as he goes to the ball.
4. Feed 2, who flashes up to the Shoulder spot after 4 moves across the lane. At this point the Jug set has been reestablished, with the change of original personnel at the Cork and at one Shoulder.

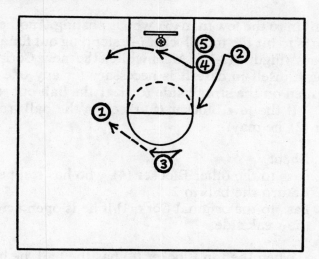

Figure 2-9

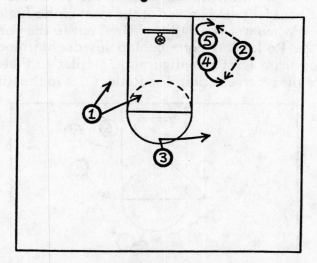

Figure 2-10

In Figure 2-10 other options occur at the end of the Pick-Roll phase of the reverse action when the Roller (2) gets the ball behind the double block. He has an option similar to the Runner's in the basic Jug action—dumping the ball in to the low man (5), who is posting. Another pass option is to hit the top Blocker (4), stepping out for a clear-out pass (Figure (2-10). Meanwhile, the new Cork (3) is freeing himself in case it is necessary for any one of the three men on the strong side to clear the ball out to him.

If the low Blocker (5) receives the ball from the Roller (2), he may:

1. Shoot.
2. Pass to the other Blocker (4), who has stepped out.
3. Return the ball to 2.
4. Pass to the original Cork (1) if he is open across on the weak side.

When the top Blocker (4) has the ball, he has the same options available to a Shoulder after the initial Cork–Shoulder pass is made at the start of the Jug action.

Whenever the ball is cleared out to the Cork spot after the Roller has gone behind his double block, the Jugging team is in a configuration similar to that at the start of the reverse action. The Roller (2) is in the Runner's

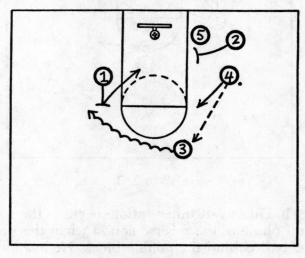

Figure 2-11

spot, the upper man (4) in the double block is near the strong-side Shoulder's position, and the former Cork (1) is at a low rebounding spot on the weak side. When the ball is in the hands of the new Cork (3), the original Cork (1) comes up to screen for him, and a new Pick-Roll series has started (Figure 2-11).

OVERLOAD REVERSE ACTION

This action is simpler than the Pick-Roll and does not open the variety of options found in the latter. It is easier to learn because it is so similar to the basic Jug movement to the strong side.

At the completion of the basic Jug action with the Blocker (5) down low, the Runner (4) on the baseline with the ball, the strong-side Shoulder (3) flared out a bit from his starting spot, and the weak-side Shoulder (2) in a rebounding spot, the ball is moved out to the Cork. The Blocker (5) follows the path of the ball from Runner to Shoulder to Cork stepping out toward each new location of the ball with the intent of receiving a pass from one of these three players. The three ball handlers should look in to him and feed him if he is open.

To start the Overload reverse action (Figure 2-12), the Cork passes to the weak-side low man (2), who V-cuts coming up the lane and out wide to receive the ball. The Blocker (5) continues to follow the ball movement and finishes his boxing of the free throw lane area by stopping near the brick on the ball side. If he has not received the ball during his moves, he becomes a Blocker for the Runner (4), who comes across the lane (as he did in the initial Jug action).

The Runner, prior to his new run, had dropped in to replace the Blocker when he moved up the lane in quest of the ball. The Runner was ready to rebound for shots by

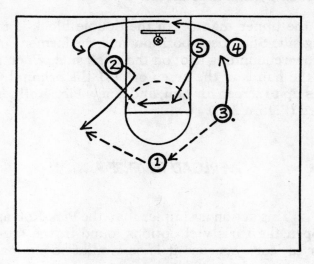

Figure 2-12

the Shoulder, the Blocker, or the Cork. He starts his new run when it is apparent that the Shoulder on the other side of the court is not going to pass to the Blocker cutting toward the baseline. He goes around the block on the new strong side, and the Overload reverse action has been completed. The former strong-side Shoulder (3) drops in to rebound, and this completes the reversal of the weak- and strong-side sets.

COMBINING PICK-ROLL AND THE OVERLOAD REVERSE ACTIONS

The continuity in the Jug offense, using either of the reverse actions, is simple once a team has mastered the reverse action. The team that pick-rolls can continue this method of reversing. The Overload-reversing team can stay with its method.

Some teams are skilled enough to exploit defensive weaknesses and take advantage of their own offensive strengths by mixing the reverse actions. The Jugsters may use one of the reverse actions and, in the continuity, follow it with the other reverse action. Another variation is to use one of the reverses in the first half and then change to the other in the second half. Alternating reverse actions each time up the court on offense is also possible.

If you plan to use both reverse actions, you must be sure your team can handle them. Confusion on the part of just one player in the Jug will take away much of its effectiveness.

OPTIONS JUST PRIOR TO REVERSE ACTION

If no shot materializes on the strong side after the first Jug movement, the Cork may decide not to initiate the Pick-Roll or the Overload when the ball is passed back out to him to start the reverse action. Instead he may decide to go back to the strong side with the ball by passing it back to the Shoulder (Figure 2-13). Another possibility is a pass

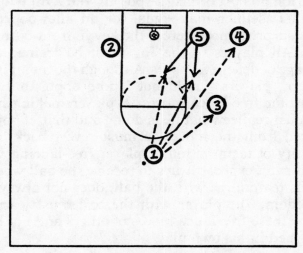

Figure 2-13

to the Blocker (5), who takes advantage of an opening and posts up. A third option for the Cork is a long pass to the Runner (2), who is momentarily open as the zone slides back toward the weak side when the ball is cleared out to the Cork. A fake pass to the weak side helps set up this option. Here the Cork displays his court sense. He reacts to the movement of the defense and consequent moves of his teammates.

If no shot occurs after the Cork's return of the ball to the strong side, the ball should come out again to him for the reverse action.

FREE-LANCING WITHIN THE JUG

Frequently while using the Jug, a team finds its opponents falling into the habit of automatically setting up to defense the expected 1-2-2 line-up. Jugsters are encouraged to take full advantage of this defensive error. The Cork looks for his chance to drive in; a Shoulder may flash to a high post or take a spot just out a bit wider than usual; a Baseliner may signal for an alley-oop pass or make a surprise move across the key in front of the hoop.

All players in the Jug must be trained to take advantage of defensive lapses. Although the intent is to run a pattern, players should not ignore opportunities that open up for free-lance moves. A player making his own move must realize what he is doing and that, if nothing is produced from the move, he must revert back into the continuity of team action. A player free-lancing without the ball can't expect always to receive the ball when he is free. His teammate, with the ball, does not always sense his freedom. The player with the ball must learn to be alert for these free-lance moves of others and not become stereotyped in his own play.

In the early training of a Jugging team you should severely limit free-lancing and concentrate on instilling the basic offense. When the fundamentals of the Jug are mastered, you may introduce more options to individuals, which will enliven the offense and motivate the players.

3

EXPANDING THE JUG

THE CORK–SHOULDER PASS

As soon as players become proficient in running the Jug in practices and the token defense against it is stepped up to full strength, it becomes evident to the Juggers that the start of the offense is based primarily on the success of the Cork–Shoulder pass. Hard work at perfecting this important facet of the offense is a must.

If the Cork does not get off his pass to a Shoulder, most of the Jug presented to this point is nullified. Aside from the Cork taking an outside shot or driving inside, the pass is the first movement of the ball into the basic Jug. This pass can be an assist leading to a field goal by the Shoulder or, in most cases, it is the key to getting the offense into gear.

Astute opponents soon realize that they must make every effort to prevent this pass. The Jugging team, therefore, must spend a lot of time in practice working not only on the techniques of the various passes used by the Cork, but also on the coordinated work of the Cork–Shoulders triangle in polishing techniques to ease movement of the ball between the two spots. The Cork's pass is usually a two-handed overhead one, but it may be a flip off the dribble, a side-arm, or even a chest pass. All Corks and Shoulders, who frequently replace the Cork, must spend time working on these passes. Passing drills using the Cork–Shoulders triangle against defense are beneficial. You must discourage overuse of the chest pass in practice drills in which little or no defense is used. Here the pass may be successful; in a game it rarely goes.

PICK FOR THE CORK

One simple action by the Cork and a Shoulder when the defense is giving the Cork difficulty is a screen by the Shoulder for the dribbling Cork. After the Cork dribbles by the screen, each of the two players takes on the responsibilities of his new position. The Cork with the ball is now the Shoulder even though he may not have penetrated as far as the normal Shoulder spot, and the former Shoulder assumes the safety and outlet duties of the cork. This interchange is simple and can be done effectively when the Cork is being hounded by a tight defensive man.

If this switch of players puts a team at a rebounding disadvantage, a reswitch after the ball goes inside to a Baseliner alleviates the situation. This is similar to the reswitch in the Pick-Roll reverse action when it is desirable to keep the Cork back on top at his normal spot. As the Jug offense continues and the team goes into a Pick-Roll reverse action, the original Cork, now at a Shoulder, will come out to assume his Cork duties as the Pick-Roll takes place; so a reswitch may not be necessary to gain offensive rebound strength.

The Baseliners must be alert to the possibility of the Shoulder picking for the Cork. When this occurs, the strong side has been established, and the Runner should start his move as the pick gets underway.

THE BASELINER–SHOULDER EXCHANGE

Another simple adjustment to aid the execution of the Cork–Shoulder pass is the trading of spots by the Baseliners and Shoulders. This change will present taller targets for the Cork to hit at the Shoulder spots, the normal Baseliners being bigger than the Shoulders. Depending on the sizes of the players in these positions, this type of trade might be done with all four front-line players or with two on only one side of the court. The trade is questionable if a height disadvantage develops as a result at the Baseliner spot or spots.

THE SHOULDER RELEASE

When the Cork gets stuck with the ball, the Shoulders must be ready to act as release men. If the Cork has used his dribble and is tied up fighting the 5-second count, he depends on the Shoulders moving out to him or even beyond him to get free for a release pass. After the release pass is made, the ball may be returned to the Cork and normal Jug spots resumed, or the release man may take over as Cork and start the offense. The former Cork then takes his spot at a Shoulder.

THE SHOULDER HIGH POST

Posting high by one Shoulder is a method of opening a lane for the starting pass of the offense. The designated Shoulder jumps out to a place near the top of the key to receive a high pass from the Cork. The other Shoulder crosses the key heading low and looking for the

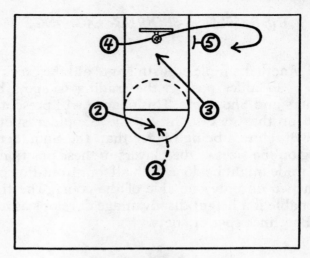

Figure 3-1

ball (Figure 3-1). If he doesn't receive the ball from the high post, he takes 4's weak-side rebound spot, and 4 becomes the Runner. He goes around the Blocker looking for a pass from the high post (Figure 3-1). The high posting Shoulder looks inside for his passing options, and the Jug action is on. The only change in assignments has been in the switching of responsibilities by the two Shoulders. If the post clears the ball back out to the Cork, he must move over to the strong side so as not to clog up the middle during the reverse action.

THE SHOULDER FLEX

Flexing the Shoulder is another way to open the Cork–Shoulder passing lane. The designated Shoulder takes a position 6 to 8 feet wider than usual (Figure 3-2), or he "jumps" to the new spot after lining up in his normal Jug spot and then moves when the Cork is ready to pass.

The flexing sets up a different angle for the pass and causes the defense to expand. This aids a Cork who is harassed by the front line of defense. Because it is easier to hit the flexed Shoulder than the normal Shoulder, the Baseliners anticipate the pass to the flexed side, and the blocking and running action of the Jug takes place just as the Cork–Shoulder pass is made.

If during the Flex the Cork can't pass to the wide Shoulder, the Blocker (4) comes up the lane into the area opened up by the flexing of the Shoulder (Figure 3-2). He often can get a turn-around shot after receiving the Cork's pass. If he doesn't shoot, he may use one of his passing options: to the weak-side rebounder (3), to the Runner (5), who has moved into the former Blocker's low-post spot, or to the flexed Shoulder (2), who finds an open spot as he drops down into the Runner spot on the baseline. This back door opening is frequently there for 2, who has been overplayed by the defense in its efforts to stop the Cork–Shoulder pass (Figure 3-2).

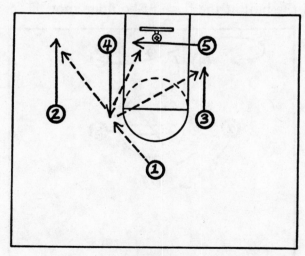

Figure 3-2

THE CORK SLANT

A variation of the Flex is the Cork Slant, in which the Cork follows his pass to the flexed Shoulder with a diagonal cut away from the ball and to a baseline weakside rebounding spot (Figure 3-3). The unflexed Shoulder slices across the lane off the Cork's tail while the off-side Baseliner (5) is running around the block on the ball side. The flexed Shoulder, with the ball, looks for passes to the other Shoulder (3) coming across the lane toward him and to the Baseliners down low on the strong side. Whether or not he uses one of his pass options, he dribbles outside, becomes the new Cork (as shown in Figure 3-3), and assumes the job of safety man and initiator of the reverse action. If the Shoulder Flex has been called, there is no need for any extra call or signal to inform the team that the Slant is going to be run. The key is the action of the Cork. If he stays after his pass, the action is the ordinary Flex; if he slants, the unflexed Shoulder reacts by slicing toward the ball at the flexed Shoulder spot.

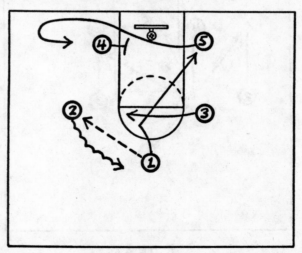

Figure 3-3

THE CORK THROUGH

This variation differs from the Slant in that the Baseliner must be signaled or alerted beforehand to hold his spot. In the normal Flex, he would be the Runner. In going through, the Cork becomes the Runner, and he goes around the block on the flexed side of the court. The man at the unflexed Shoulder spot replaces at the Cork spot (Figure 3-4). Note that the flexed Shoulder (2) might be able to pass to the Cork as he is going through before he goes around the block.

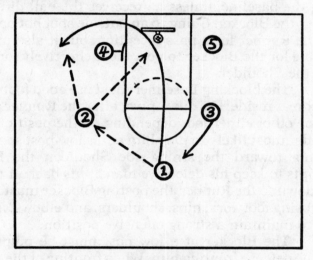

Figure 3-4

SOLVING BASELINE PROBLEMS

After the Jug has been run against a zoning team, it is often necessary for the Baseliners to do some adjusting to cause more trouble for the defensive back line. Often the back defender nearest the Baseliner who becomes the

Runner will step off toward the baseline with the Runner in an attempt to take away that route. The Runner in that case pushes off his outside (baseline-side) foot and cuts back over the *top* of the block.

The Runner should not attempt to take the baseline route each time he goes around the block. He can keep the defense honest if he occasionally goes directly over the top of the block. If the defense reacts to this move by playing the Runner higher, the Runner will find that the baseline route is now opened up (Figure 3-4).

Regardless of his path, high or low, around the block the Runner must continue going to an outside spot along the baseline, unless he receives the ball directly in front of the Blocker. Going to an outside spot not only may free the Runner for a pass reception, but it also makes it possible for the Blocker to post more effectively for a pass from the Shoulder.

The blocking Baseliner must use good footwork to be a threat inside. His quick pivot after the Runner goes by may be off of either foot depending on the position of the defender most likely to play him at his low-post spot. After pivoting toward the strong-side Shoulder, the Blocker attempts to keep his defensive man at his back. If the ball goes down to the Runner, the posting Blocker must manipulate using footwork, hips, shoulders, and elbows, if necessary, to maintain a strong offensive position.

The Blocker at a low post must be prepared to find the defense fronting him. When fronting of the posting Blocker occurs, the Shoulder should consider the lob pass inside over the defense. If a low weak-side defender shifts over toward the post to help against the lob threat, the Jug's weak-side rebounder may be open for the pass from the Shoulder. The rebounder receiving a pass from the Shoulder may get the good percentage shot near the basket, or he may be able to hit the Cork at an open spot behind the front-line defense on the weak side (Figure 3-5).

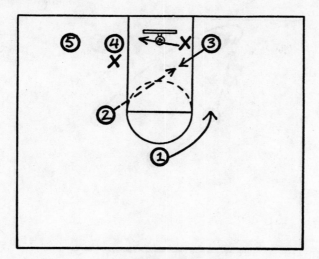

Figure 3-5

THE DISLOCATED SHOULDER

When a team is able to run the basic Jug with at least one of the reverse actions in the continuity until a shot results, it is time to add a few variations to the basic pattern. One of the first, and probably the most elementary, is the *Dislocate,* in which a Shoulder cuts diagonally low around the Baseliner's block (Figure 3-6). This Shoulder actually assumes the Runner's route in this variation. The Baseliner (5) who normally would be the Runner stays as the weak-side rebounder. A Shoulder who is a good medium-distance shooter now gets a crack at his shot from a different spot on the court. The Dislocate helps the Baseliners on smaller teams to gain important rebound positions.

This Dislocate move of the Shoulder becomes effective when the back line of the defense has become

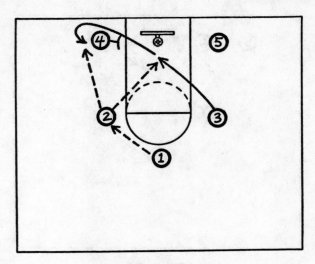

Figure 3-6

used to the regular Jug action of the Baseliners and then is suddenly confronted with a new challenge. Sometimes the cut by the Shoulder is such a surprise that he is open as he cuts across the lane even before reaching the block (Figure 3-6). The feeding Shoulder (2) should look for this option first.

Over the years players using the Dislocate have abbreviated the term to "Kate"; and eventually it wound up as K, a much easier call than the three-syllable word "dislocate."

To minimize confusion when K is on, there must be a definite way of informing the entire team that this brand of the Jug is being run. Several methods have been used: a signal or verbal call from the bench, a call or signal during play by the Cork or another player responsible for the offense, or a call by the coach in a time-out huddle or during the pregame or half-time talk. Teams that use the huddle prior to a free throw may decide on its use at that time.

There are several ways to run the Dislocate. Without predetermination the Cork may set the dislocate side by his pass alone. The Shoulder not receiving the ball becomes the dislocator and the Baseliners, knowing that K is on, are prepared to block for whichever Shoulder takes the diagonal cut. Another means of designating the dislocator is by a signal from the Cork, who waves his free hand to the side he prefers or merely dribbles to that side.

A Shoulder can be selected as the player who indicates the side where K will be run. By placing a hand on his hip he can show whether he or the other Shoulder will dislocate. His inside hand on his hip with the elbow pointing at his fellow Shoulder shows that the other Shoulder dislocates. The Cork then works to get his pass to the man who is signaling. In this manner the dislocator may anticipate his cut. Conversely, the outside hand on hip means that the signaler will dislocate. The absence of hand on hip tells the Cork to use his own discretion. Then the Cork's pass is the key to the side the play goes.

A coach wishing to exploit the shooting ability of one of his Shoulders may have that man always dislocate—and, in order not to limit the offense to just one side of the court, allow that one player to change sides at the Shoulder spots at random times when the Jug line-up is initially set up. The other Shoulder lines up in the initial set at the Shoulder spot left open by the shooter–dislocator Shoulder.

THE T MOVE

The T, so called because of the formation made by the movement of the Shoulders to the baseline, is another variation from the basic Jug. When the signal for this action is given, the Shoulders know that they are going to peel off to the outside and take positions along the baseline about 15 feet from the basket. The movement is timed to coincide with the Cork's crossing of the mid-court line (Figure 3-7). The Baseliners' function is to block their

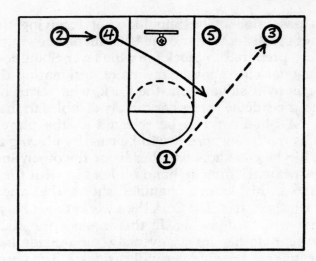

Figure 3-7

defensive men so that they can't go directly out to pick up the Shoulders in their new spots along the baseline. The Cork's pass to a Shoulder is longer than in the basic Jug, but often it is easier to make. If the passing lanes are closed by quick defensive adjustment to the new move of the Shoulders, the Baseliners flash up the lane looking for the Cork's pass. In this case the Shoulders, now on the baseline, close in, taking normal Baseliner spots. The basic Jug set has been reestablished.

In T, when a Shoulder on the baseline receives the ball from the Cork, his options are: (1) make a shot; (2) dump the ball in to the Baseliner posting low, (3) pass to the off-side Baseliner coming across to assume his new job as a Shoulder on the ball side, and (4) clear out to the Cork (Figure 3-7). If the ball comes back out to the Cork, the reverse action is started.

THE CURL

The Curl is similar to the T move, but in this phase of the Jug, the Shoulders, instead of flaring back to wide baseline spots, curl down and head-hunt for the defensive men nearest the Baseliners. The Baseliners pop out around the picks of the shoulders to free themselves for the Cork's pass (Figure 3-8). The Cork attempts to get the ball to a moving Baseliner—not after the Baseliner stops his cut. The same options occur as in T if the pass is made to the cutting Baseliner. If the pass is not made, the Shoulders flash up the lane just as the Baseliners do in T, and the popped-out Baseliners resume their original spots. The team is now back in its basic Jug formation.

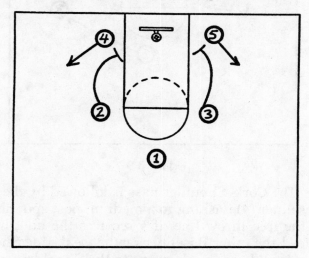

Figure 3-8

The Curl will loosen up the zone that is concentrating on stopping the Cork–Shoulder pass. Now it must concern itself with two other receivers coming within better passing range of the Cork.

BEAN POT

To change the look of the offense and to open other passing lanes, the jug is widened at the Shoulders to put it in the Bean Pot set. Bean Pot may be started with the

Shoulders taking their new spots farther out on an imaginary extension of the free throw line or with the Shoulders assuming their basic spot and then jumping out (Jumping Bean Pot) to their new positions (Figure 3-9).

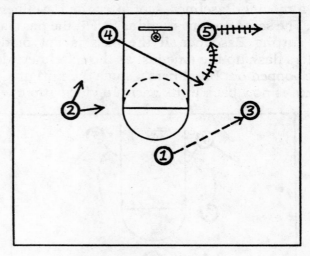

Figure 3-9

The Cork–Shoulder pass is followed by the weakside Baseliner (4) flashing to a medium-post spot near the end of the free throw line. If 4 receives the ball, he may shoot, feed the other Baseliner or the weak-side Shoulder who dropped down, or clear out to the Shoulder or to the Cork. Player 3, the Shoulder who receives the Cork's pass, has another passing option—the Baseliner low on his side of the court (Figure 3-9).

If the Shoulder does not pass to the medium post, the low post (strong-side Baseliner, 5) steps out along the baseline, looking for a pass. The medium post (4) goes down the lane ready to receive the ball from the Shoulder or from the Baseliner if he has the ball. If the Shoulder retains the ball, the normal Overload triangle of the Jug has been established, and the usual clearing out and reverse action follow.

The adjustment of some zones to the Bean Pot may open up the middle of the court for a drive by a Cork talented enough to get inside. The opening of the middle, which causes the defense to expand, also allows a release action by a Baseliner who, when the Shoulders are contained by the defense, breaks to a high-post spot in the top of the key for a pass from the Cork. Both Shoulders cut toward the basket as the remaining Baseliner crosses in front of the basket (Figure 3-10).

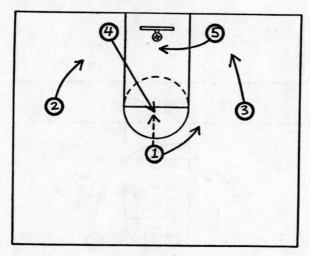

Figure 3-10

When the high-posting Baseliner (4) receives the ball, he faces the basket, looking for his own shot; for his partner coming across in front of the hoop; for the Shoulders cutting toward the basket; and for the Cork who floats to the weak side. If he uses none of these options, he clears out to the Cork or to the weak-side Shoulder and goes down the lane replacing the Baseliner (5), who has stepped out along the baseline (Figure 3-11). The continuity now becomes the same as in the Bean Pot.

After the high-post release, a different continuity may be substituted. Instead of using a clear-out to the Cork

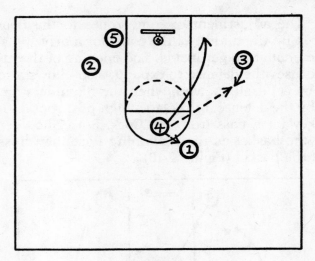

Figure 3-11

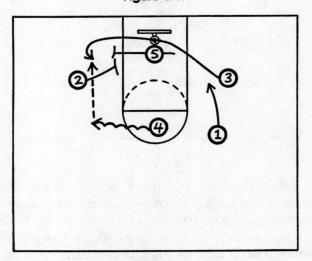

Figure 3-12

or Shoulder, the high post looks for the weak-side Shoulder (3) coming around the double screen formed by the Baseliner and the strong-side Shoulder. This action is very similar to the final part of the Pick-Roll reverse action (Figure 3-12).

If the Pick-Roll reverse action is not the one used by a team when it is in the basic Jug, the Overload reverse action may be used as the follow-up to the high-post release of the Bean Pot. The post clears out to the Cork or to the strong-side Shoulder and follows the ball around the horn in the usual manner of this reverse action.

SUMMARY

Several variations of the Jug—Dislocate, Flex, T, Curl, Bean Pot—have been presented in this chapter along with different wrinkles within the variations. It is asking a lot of a team to master all of them, especially if the team is in its first season of Jugging. The prudent coach will select those parts of the offense that fit his philosophy and can be digested by his team. He must emphasize in practice sessions the importance of perfecting the Cork–Shoulder pass, and he must train his players in the techniques used to aid in the execution of this key to the start of the Jug offense.

4

STICK A FLOWER IN THE JUG

There is a story about an old hillbilly who fooled the investigating federal agents on his place by opening his jugs of moonshine and sticking flowers in them. A basketball team uses the same tactic when it runs the Jug offense from an initial set other than the 1-2-2 formation. By camouflaging the Jug, a team gives the defense the impression that it is looking at something different. The only differences are in the starting formation and a few options peculiar to particular sets. As with the moonshiner's jug, it may look different, but it's the same basic stuff with the same effect.

Bean Pot, a "flower" already covered in the preceding chapter, is run from a set made different by the widening of the Shoulders. In essence it is only a slight variation from the basic 1-2-2. It is still a 1-2-2, but against odd-front zones, Bean Pot usually opens up the middle as the defense expands to try to cover the Shoulders at their new spots. A clever Cork can take advantage of this expansion and penetrate the shell of the defense. The Cork will have different passing lanes to the Shoulders, and he will find it easier to pass to the Baseliners. Other than these changes and the flashing of the Baseliner to a medium-post spot, the balance of the offense is strictly basic Jug action. Most of the other "flowers" in the Jug are of similar nature.

R-RIGHT, L-LEFT

When the Shoulder spot on one side of the court is filled by both Shoulders standing side by side, the Jug is given a different appearance (Figure 4-1). When it's done on the right side, it is called R. If the defense does not make an immediate adjustment to this change, the outside Shoulder will be open for the Cork's pass. The inside Shoulder helps by blocking any defensive man in the area.

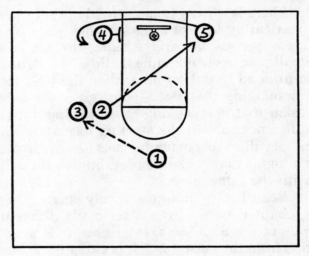

Figure 4-1

The outside Shoulder continues the Jug offense by shooting or passing to any of his usual receivers. The weak-side Baseliner becomes the Runner, and the inside Shoulder slants away from the ball to go to his weak-side rebounding position (Figure 4-1). The same formation used on the other side of the court (the left) is called L.

If in R or L the Cork passes to the weak-side Baseliner, who may move up the lane to free himself, the Overload reverse action is on. But if the Cork dribbles in on an angle to the weak side, the Baseliner comes up to Pick and Roll, and *that* reverse action is on. In the latter case, the outside Shoulder balances the floor at the Cork spot, and the inside Shoulder drops down the lane to form the double screen (Figure 4-2).

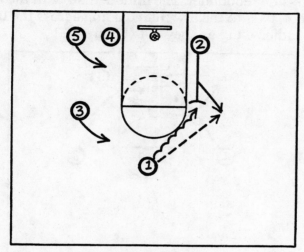

Figure 4-2

If the defense prevents the pass to the outside Shoulder, the inside Shoulder may find an open spot across the lane at the weak-side Shoulder spot. If he receives the ball, normal Jug action follows, with the Runner going around the block on the side of the ball.

1-3-1

That old favorite formation for fighting zones, the 1-3-1, may be used as part of the Jug. A team that normally uses a 1-3-1 offense may wish to incorporate the Jug into their regular offense. When a team is Jugging from it, the moves are as follows.

The pass from the Cork to the middle man keys a quick dart across in front of the basket by the low man (5). At the same time, the wings start cutting to the basket. The wing on 5's side continues through and across the lane as the Runner. The other wing (2) goes across to become the weak-side rebounder. The middle man with the ball (4) may shoot, pass to the low man darting across the lane, or pass to either wing as they cut (Figure 4-3).

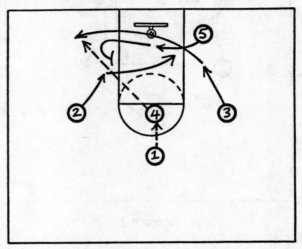

Figure 4-3

The pass to the Runner coming around the block develops later as a wing goes around the low man's block. If none of these options are taken, the middle man should look for the Cork, who may have found an opening on the weak-side wing area. A clear-out to the Cork merely sets up the reverse action phase of the Jug.

From the 1-3-1 formation, a point-to-wing pass on the strong side (the side where the low man sets) keys a Jug move (Figure 4-4) to that side, with the middle man becoming the Runner around the low man's block. The

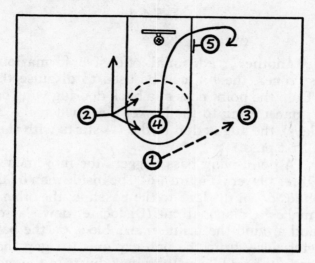

Figure 4-4

weak-side wing looks for penetrating gaps before assuming weak-side rebounding duties.

A point-to-weak-side wing pass keys a roll down the lane by the middle man and the low man's run across the lane (Figure 4-5).

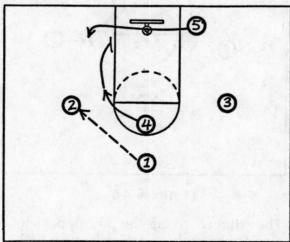

Figure 4-5

THE 1-4

Another traditional offensive formation used against zones, the 1-4, can be used to disguise the Jug. Aside from the point pass to a back-dooring wing or to an inside man rolling to the basket (used when the defense overplays), the Jug action in the 1-4 starts with the point man's first pass.

A point-wing pass triggers the movement of the other three players (Figure 4-6). The inside man on the ball side slides down the lane to the baseline; the other inside man makes a diagonal cut (Dislocate) down across the lane and around the inside man's block on the ball side. The wing away from the ball explores the gap that may develop in the middle as the zone adjusts to the moves on the ball side. After gapping, the wing goes in to rebound.

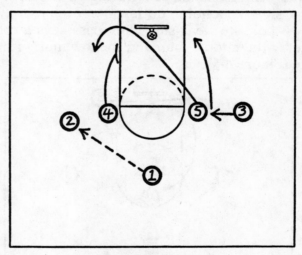

Figure 4-6

The wing receiving the point's pass looks for his shot first and then to his passing options: (1) the inside man going down the lane, (2) the dislocator during his diagonal cut in the lane, and (3) the opposite wing filling the hole left when the inside men leave their spots. His next passing options are the usual Jug alternatives: Dislocator around the block, Blocker posting low, weak-side rebounder flashing, and Cork outside for the clear-out.

A point-inside man pass (Figure 4-7) means that the other inside man makes the Dislocate move, the ball-side wing cuts to the brick looking for the ball and then blocks for the dislocator, and the wing away from the ball gaps and then goes inside to rebound on his side of the court. To make the pass to the dislocator coming around the block, the insider with the ball may have to dribble to the side to get a better passing angle.

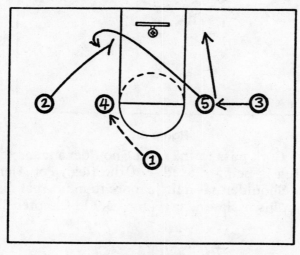

Figure 4-7

HALF A BEAN POT (RIGHT OR LEFT)

As the name implies, this set is in the form of a Bean Pot on one side, achieved by one Shoulder playing out wide while the other is in normal Jug position. The Cork's pass to the wide Shoulder signifies that Bean Pot is on. The only difference from the normal Bean Pot is that the weak-side Shoulder is in tighter; however, he retains his job of getting the off-side rebound position (Figure 4-8).

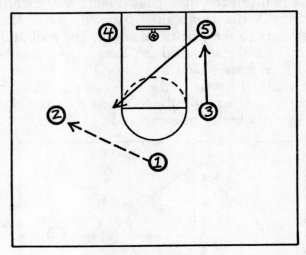

Figure 4-8

A Cork pass to the tight Shoulder means that the regular Jug is being played, not the Bean Pot. Here, the wide-side Shoulder has a little more than normal distance to cover in his assignment (Figure 3-9 in Chapter 3).

THE DOUBLE STACK

Pushing each Shoulder down so he is stacked up with his respective Baseliner gives a new look to the Jug (Figure 4-9). The initial moves by the bottom players in the stack are the same as those used by them in the popular Scramble man-for-man offense that uses this set. They banana up to what are regular Jug Shoulder spots, moving out as the Cork crosses the 10-second line to start the

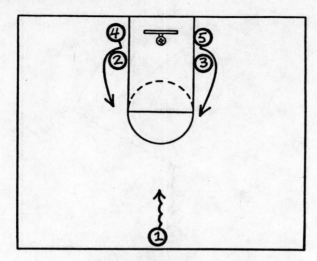

Figure 4-9

action. The Cork then has two potential receivers moving up toward him. Should the defense pack in against this formation, the bottom men may flare out into a wider spread, and the Bean Pot has been established.

If a team loses much rebounding strength by stacking Shoulders on top of Baseliners, the players assigned to these spots may be switched during the Double Stack so that the bottom men who come out to the Shoulder spots are the actual assigned Shoulders of the team.

If a team is trained in free-lance play, it may, while running the Jug from the Double Stack, key on the paths of the bottom men when they come up to meet the Cork's pass. The Bean Pot is used when the bottom men flare (or in the case of Half a Bean Pot, when one man flares—Figure 4-10) and the pass is to the flared man. The regular Jug is used when the bottom men come out straight or the straight man has been hit and the other bottom man has flared. If your team is not comfortable with this type of free-lancing, you can designate which type of Jug will be run from the Double Stack.

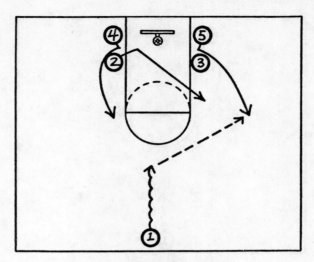

Figure 4-10

THE TRIPLE STACK

In order to cut down on confusion, the three-man stack on one side of the lane is made of: the Baseliner on that side of the court in the bottom spot; the Shoulder from that side in the top spot; and in the middle, a player the coach chooses on the basis of the comparative strengths and weaknesses of the two men normally on the other side of the lane.

The lone man on the nonstacked side may play low or in normal Baseliner position. In that case it might be simplest to assign that spot to the player who usually is the Baseliner on that side of the court. The loner may be spotted anywhere along the lane line.

The Cork judges his actions according to the zone he faces. If the defense has skewed to the stacked side, there may be room for him to play some two-man ball with loner (4) on the weak side. A Pick-Roll action similar to the usual reverse action or a pass to the loner coming out for a quick shot may work.

If a pass to the loner does not produce a shot (Figure 4-11), the top man of the stack slants to the Baseliner spot on the weak side. (He may be open as he goes.) The bottom man on the stack runs across around the Baseliner's block to go into Jug action.

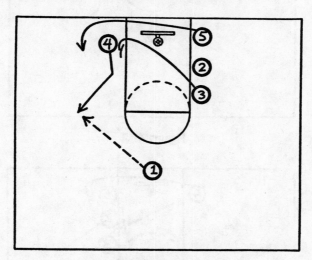

Figure 4-11

A Pick-Roll play by the Cork and the loner is followed by the usual continuity in the Jug, with the top stack man becoming the new Cork.

Whenever the loner plays up at the Shoulder spot or flashes up to that spot, another option opens up. The bottom man may jump across the lane (Figure 4-12) to the spot vacated by 4, and the Cork may lob the ball to him. This move may be used as a set play in a special situation.

When using the Triple Stack, the Cork should look first for the middle-stack man (2) popping out to the side (Figure 4-13). The top and bottom men in the stack attempt to block the defense from getting outside to stop the popper. Following the pass to the popper, if no shot is

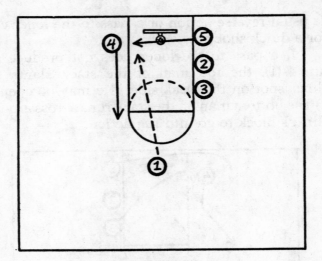

Figure 4-12

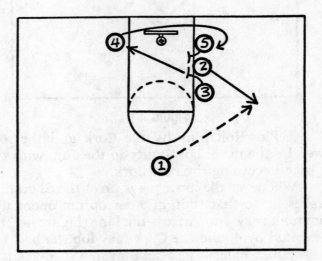

Figure 4-13

taken, the top man on the stack goes diagonally across the lane down to the off-side rebound spot while the loner comes across the key as the Runner. The Runner goes around the bottom stacker's block in normal Jug fashion.

If the pass to the middle man (Figure 4-13) popping out is not made, the Cork may want to hit the top man on the stack—the Shoulder (3). If so, the middle man (2) turns down into the bottom man (5) and blocks for him as he steps out along the baseline. Whether there is an actual block or not, the stepping out of the bottom man signals that the Jugging has started.

TWO CORKS

The set for Two Corks is a 2-3 formation with two guards out and a front line with the middle man in the top of the key and the wings out on the free throw line extended (Figure 4-14). Starting the offense with a guard-to-guard pass makes for better timing. Preferably, the passer cuts *behind* the high-post man and goes around a block by the ball-side wing, who has moved to the brick on the free throw lane. This wing, on seeing the guard-to-

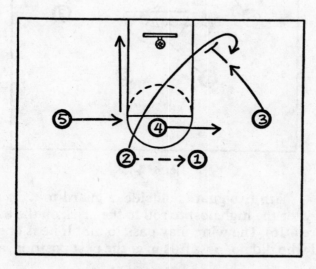

Figure 4-14

guard pass, cuts to the brick, looking for a possible pass from the guard. The weak-side wing drops in to rebound, after first checking the possibility of a move to a gap on the weak side. The middle man (high post) becomes the strong-side Shoulder. He may have to move out of the free throw circle to receive the pass from the guard (Cork). The Double Cork has now turned into the normal Jug.

From the starting 2-3 set, a guard-to-high-post pass results in a diagonal cut to the hoop by the nonfeeding guard (2) (Figure 4-15). The post (4) looks for both wings cutting to the bricks, for 2 cutting through, and for his own shot. If there are no openings, 4 dribbles to the sides from which the pass came and attempts to get the ball to the guard coming around the block on the ball side. Again, the usual Jug Overload positions are filled.

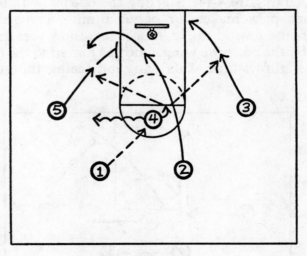

Figure 4-15

With two guards outside, a guard-to-wing pass is the key for the high post to roll to the brick on the ball side (Figure 4-16). The wing may pass to him if he is open. The guard who did not pass fills in at the post position, and the

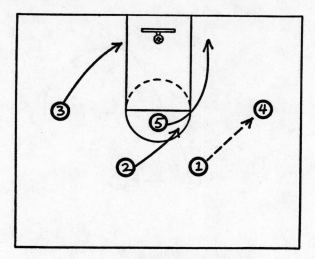

Figure 4-16

weak-side wing takes off-side rebound responsibilities. If the wing can't hit the roller or the guard filling the post, he clears out to the Cork. Now the formation is the same as it would be at the end of Bean Pot, and the Jug offense continues from that point.

THE 2-1-2

The 2-1-2, with two guards, a high post, and two forwards pinched in low, is treated in the same manner as the 2-3 set. The guard-to-guard pass (Figure 4-17) elicits a break-out by the forward on the ball side, but if he does not receive the ball, he goes down to the brick to block for the cutting guard, just as in the 2-3. The guard-to-post pass may be easier to make than in the 2-3 if the defense plays back deeper on the low forwards. The guard-to-wing pass, most times, will go only if the forwards free themselves by a quick move out to wing spots.

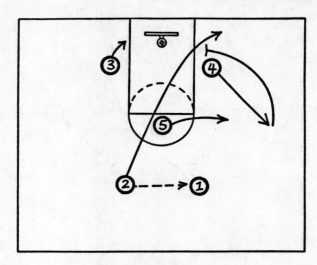

Figure 4-17

KEEP IT SIMPLE

The hillbilly who fooled the "revenooers" probably didn't use a great variety of flowers. A basketball team doesn't have to disguise its Jug by using all the sets described here. As is the case in selecting types of Jug variations (see Chapter 3), the use of different sets to confuse opponents should be limited by the experience and the skill of the Jugging team. The more limited a team is, the simpler the "flowers" should be in the cover-up of the intended offensive action.

It might seem logical to use a disguise set with which a team is already familiar because it was used previously for zone or man-for-man offenses. However, consideration must be given to the possible negative transfer effect often inherent in cases where old habits have to be replaced by new ones. Whether to use a familiar set or not to hide the Jug comes down to your deciding what your team can best handle.

The R-Right, L-Left formation might be your choice if you have a 3 (Figure 4-1) who hits well from the outside spot and can get his shot off quickly.

If your team runs a 1-3-1 or 1-4 offense, the flowers these formations provide (Figures 4-3, 4-4 and 4-5) may be the way to disguise your Jug. Similarly, if you have your team run a stack offense against man defense, you may want to consider Jugging from the Double Stack (Figures 4-9 and 4-10) or from the Triple Stack (Figures 4-11, 4-12, and 4-13).

Using Two Corks (Figures 4-14, 4-15, and 4-16) and/ or the 2-1-2 flower (Figure 4-17) may be the way to go if your team runs an offense that employs two guards and three men up front.

5

BEATING
THE EVEN-FRONT
ZONES

SPLIT THE TWO-MAN FRONT

In attacking all two-man fronts, the Cork must bring the ball directly to an imaginary spot between the front-line defenders, or at least he should head toward that spot in order to force them to make decisions. When the ball is at that spot, the defense has three options:

1. Remain in its initial defensive line-up positions.
2. Converge on the ball (both front-line defenders).
3. Have one front-line defender take the ball.

Against the first defense option, the Cork maintains his dribble and attempts to penetrate between the two front-line defenders. If successful, he then works against the second line of defense. This option does not occur often, but it will be possible whenever the front-liners leave a gap between themselves. Often this type of error will occur the first time in a game that the opponent goes into a two-man front type defense.

In case the Cork does penetrate between the two front defenders, the Shoulders should be ready to rebound for the Cork's jump shot or to receive a dish-off from him if the second line of defense leaves them to stop the Cork. The Baseliners, too, should be ready to rebound and to receive a pass if the rear defenders move up to help against the Cork–Shoulder action. As in any Cork penetration beyond the Shoulders, the Cork must be replaced. In this case a designated Shoulder replaces him.

If both defensive front-liners converge on the ball, the Cork must pass off before he is tied up. The Shoulders must be active in this situation, giving the Cork passing lanes at a time when he can use them.

When only one of the front-liners takes the Cork, the one-on-one strength of the Cork may be utilized. The Cork looks for openings for his pass behind the man guarding him and on that defensive man's side of the court. There is also the possibility of using the Shoulder on that side to pick for the Cork.

The Shoulder who is picking for the Cork may set him up for a jumper, or at least make it easier for the Cork to pass directly to an inside man—the Runner, the posting Blocker or the flashing off-side rebounder (Figure 5-1). The picking Shoulder replaces the Cork as the safety outlet man. In Figure 5-1, F stands for front-line defender, M for middle defender, and R for rear defender.

If the front-liners hang back, a good outside-shooting Cork can fire away as the rest of his team works at getting good rebounding positions. To do this the Cork must be an excellent shooter, and his team must know that he can and will shoot over the deep sagging defense.

A Cork who is much shorter than the two front men may have a great deal of difficulty passing the ball. This may warrant substituting a taller Cork from the bench or having the Cork trade spots with a taller team-mate at one of the Shoulder spots.

In facing two-man front zones, the Jugging team must be ready to work hard during the transition from

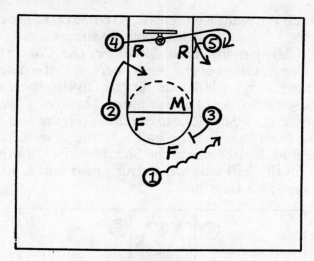

Figure 5-1

offense to defense when their opponents use the two front-liners to "cherry pick," or as primary outlet pass receivers in the start of their fast break. The Cork, as the safety, often will have to defend against two men in the transition. The Shoulders, who during the course of the Jug offense may become Corks, must be safety conscious. They, and the Baseliners, must work hard at stopping quick outlet passes whenever the ball is lost in the rebounding battle.

BASIC JUG VS. THE 2-1-2

Because the 2-1-2 is the most commonly used even-front zone, more time must be spent in practice working against it. All of the Cork's threats with the ball are used against the two front defenders (F, F)—for example, splitting the seam between them, shooting over any extreme sag, and using a Shoulder's pick.

If the Cork penetrates the front line and is picked up by the middle defender (M), he looks for a pass to a

Shoulder. If the rear defenders (R, R) come up to guard the Shoulders, he then looks for open Baseliners.

After passing to a Shoulder, the Cork should observe the reactions of the front-liners. If F, the defensive player away from the ball side, drops in to clog the middle, the Cork should attempt to free himself in order to act as a relay passer from Shoulder to Shoulder (Figure 5-2). If the defensive front-liner on the ball side drops in to double with the middle defender at the Shoulder, the Cork tries to get free on the ball side for a return pass and a possible shot or pass to a Baseliner.

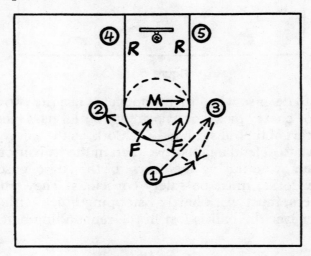

Figure 5-2

The middle defender (M) must be tested. He alone cannot adequately guard the Shoulders, both of whom are in his normal defense area. If he cheats toward one side when the Cork has the ball, the Shoulder on the other side will be left open. If he doesn't overplay one side, he must commit himself when the pass goes to a Shoulder. The pressure is on him to guard the ball in the Shoulder area. If he doesn't, he gives up, at worst, a 17-foot shot.

When the middle defender moves to the Shoulder who receives the Cork's pass, the other Shoulder is momentarily open for a quick cross-court pass. This pass (Figure 5-3) must be made before the front and rear defensive lines adjust to the ball movement.

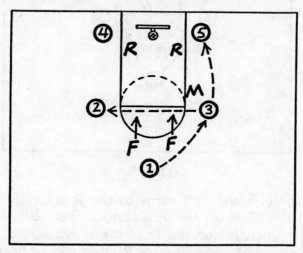

Figure 5-3

If the middle defender holds his position between the Shoulders and the rear defender on ball side moves up to guard the Shoulder with the ball, the Baseliner on that side immediately becomes open and should be hit. A shift by the middle man down to guard this Baseliner leaves the opposite Shoulder open—just as when the middle man guards the Shoulder with the ball. Whether the Shoulder passes across to the other Shoulder or to the Baseliner, he follows the rule of getting open for a return pass.

When the rear defender moves up to guard the ball at the Shoulder (Figure 5-4), the off-side front-liner may shut off the pass lane to the other Shoulder. This defensive move allows the middle defender to shift down to guard the strong-side Baseliner (4). In this case the

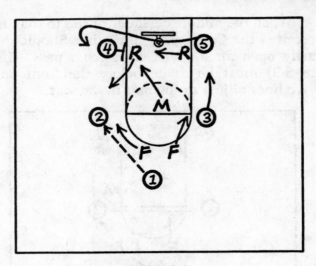

Figure 5-4

Shoulder with the ball turns to the Runner (5) coming around the block in the Jug action. The weak-side rear defender must honor the Runner's move across the key toward the ball; otherwise, the Runner will be open under the basket. This freezing of the weak-side defender means that the weak-side Shoulder can only be covered by a front-liner dropping in. A hustling front line will try to cover the middle area after the ball has gone beyond it, so quick passes are essential for the Jugging players to gain any advantage.

If the weak-side defender (W) crosses the key to guard the Blocker (4) when the strong-side defender (S) moves out to cover the Runner (5), a front-liner may slide all the way down to a spot near the basket. Frequently he is overmatched in size by the Shoulder (3) in the weak-side rebounding spot. The offense should take advantage of this by lobbing the ball over him to the Shoulder or having the Shoulder flash in front of the basket (Figure 5-5).

The openings that occur for the offense must be recognized and used as they appear. That is why it is so

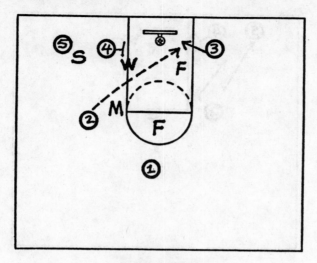

Figure 5-5

important that a pattern be followed. The Juggers maintain the edge as long as the players anticipate the openings that occur in the progression of the offense.

The "corners," particularly vulnerable in this variety of zone, are exploited by the Jug when the Runner goes around the Baseliner's block. The Runner can obtain a 10-foot shot or better if the middle defender is the one who covers him. It is difficult for this defensive man to follow the Shoulder–Runner pass quickly enough to stop the shot (Figure 5-6). If the back defender on the ball side fights around the block to take the Runner, the Runner usually will receive the ball farther out along the baseline for his shot. If he can't shoot, the inside strength of the low-posting Blocker may be used. He is fed by Runner or Shoulder.

The continuity of the Overload reverse action presents the same types of options on the other side of the court. The Pick-Roll version of reverse action (Figure 5-7) may result in a jump shot by the Cork, but seldom does the pass to the roller go against a true 2-1-2. However, the

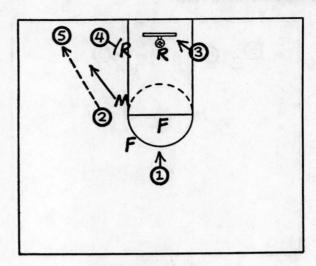

Figure 5-6

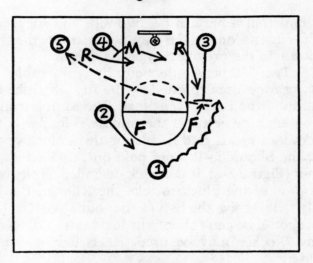

Figure 5-7

Runner is frequently left open over on the strong side of the court behind the other Baseliner. The Cork should look for this opening before clearing the ball out.

K VS. THE 2-1-2

The diagonal move of the off-side Shoulder in K, the Dislocate, gives the ball-side rear defender problems. He becomes outnumbered, and usually he won't get much immediate help from his teammates. The middle man is normally guarding the ball at the Shoulder; the front line is too far away to give much aid; and the weak-side defender is concerned with the weak-side Baseliner.

If the weak-side defender shifts over to the ball side to allow the rear defender on the ball side to go around the block to guard the dislocator, the weak-side Baseliner can flash in front of the hoop for a dump-in by the Shoulder. The weak-side Baseliner may have another option if a front-liner has dropped down to defense him (Figure 5-8). The Baseliner (4), if he is taller than the front-liner, may hold instead of flashing and call for a lob pass from the Shoulder.

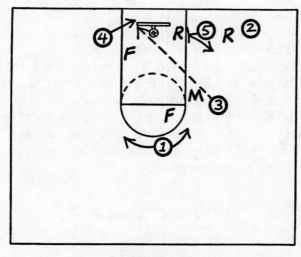

Figure 5-8

T VS. THE 2-1-2

The T move—of the two Shoulders peeling off to go to baseline spots—puts potential scorers in the "corners" (Figure 3-7 in Chapter 3) almost immediately after the Cork brings the ball into the front court. Good blocks by the Baseliners on the rear defenders plus a sharp pass from the Cork to one of the Shoulders at his new baseline position are essential. The middle defender, if he retains his normal mid-position on the court, should not be able to stop the pass. If he shifts to one side, the pass should go to the open side.

If the Shoulders don't get free or if the front-liners pick up the Cork at mid-court, the Baseliners must move up the lane as relief men. They should head for spots in the Shoulders' area where the middle defender can't simultaneously guard both of them.

CURL VS. THE 2-1-2

The action of the Shoulders curling down to spring the Baseliners is effective against the 2-1-2 (Figure 3-8 in Chapter 3). The Shoulders block out the two rear defenders, and the Baseliners come out at a slight angle so the middle defender can't stop both of them from receiving the Cork's pass. In this variation, as in the T, harassment of the Cork by the front-liners may necessitate an early Curl move to insure the completion of the pass.

BEAN POT VS. THE 2-1-2

The spread of the Shoulders in the Bean Pot virtually eliminates the middle defender. If he remains in his mid-spot, he can't bother the Cork–Shoulder pass. If he cheats toward one side (Figure 5-9), the Shoulder on the opposite side will be left even more open. Cheating this way also puts the middle defender out of position to defense the flashing weak-side Baseliner and the ball-side Baseliner.

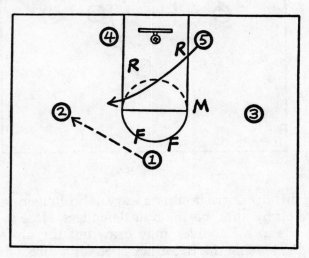

Figure 5-9

    If the rear defender on the ball side comes out to defense the Shoulder with the ball, the middle man may drop down to cover one pass away near the strong-side Baseliner (Figure 5-10). In this case the flashing weak-side Baseliner should find an open post spot before a front-liner moves down to defend the middle area. If 4 is followed out by the rear defender on the weak side, the weak-side Shoulder (2) going to the hoop will be open.

    The Cork may find that the two front-liners drop in to help against the flashing post man regardless of whether the middle defender or the rear defender covers the ball at the Shoulder. In this case the Cork starts the offense from farther out so as to lengthen the slide of the front-liners down to their secondary defensive spots. In

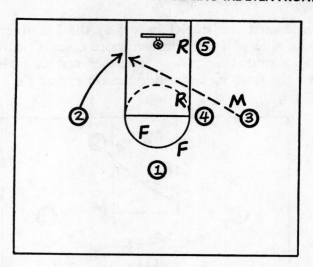

Figure 5-10

doing this the Cork should be wary of his longer pass being picked off by anticipating rear defenders. Here is where a fake pass to a Shoulder may draw out the anxious rear defender, leaving the Baseliner open for a direct pass from the Cork.

ATTACKING THE 2-3

The usual testing of the front line—attempted penetration of the front line—and the basic Jug attack, as used against the 2-1-2, are applied against the 2-3. In most ways this zone may be treated as a 2-1-2, for against the Jug it often deteriorates into the more common defense with a middle man between front and back lines.

If the back three men in this zone stay low, the Shoulders will get more than their usual share of medium shots. Unless the Shoulders are poor shooters, the additional defensive rebound strength obtained by the defense keeping three men back will be wasted. Against a deep sagging back defensive line, the Cork can use the Shoulder pick in order to obtain shots within 15 feet of the basket.

If the back defenders move up in line with the Shoulders, the Baseliners will be free to operate behind the zone. Both Cork and Shoulders should work to get the ball to the inside men.

Bean Potting the 2-3 when the rear-wing defenders guard the Shoulders puts the middle defender at a disadvantage because he will be outnumbered by the Baseliners during the flashing post play (Figure 5-11).

Against the basic Jug, a rear-wing man coming out to take the ball at the Shoulder, plus the shift of the middle man to the ball-side Baseliner, make it difficult to get the low-post shot that is sometimes easily obtained against the 2-1-2.

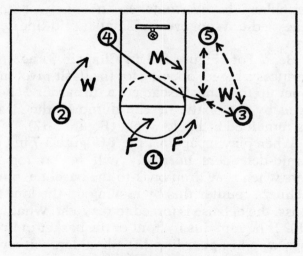

Figure 5-11

ATTACKING THE 2-2-1

Although the 2-2-1 is much rarer than either of the two other even-front zones, it is necessary for a team to be ready for the opponent who might use it—the team with personnel to pressure the Shoulders and back them up with a big goalie.

In this defense the two-man pressure put on the Cork and the matching-up at the Shoulders give it great outside strength. The weakness is underneath, even if the defense has a giant stationed there. He will be outnumbered by the two Baseliners. It takes good ball handling to get the ball to these Baseliners, so the Shoulders must be very active to free themselves for the Cork's pass.

It may pay the offense to sacrifice some size under the basket and bring their taller men to the middle by switching the Baseliners and Shoulders in order to ease the Cork–Shoulder pass. Often the 2-2-1 team has one giant plus four ordinary mortals. If the Jugging team has one big man, he might be used to better advantage at the Shoulder where he overmatches an opponent and can obtain the medium shot over his smaller mid-line defender opponent.

Bean Pot (Figure 3-9 in Chapter 3) against the 2-2-1 produces a bigger opening for the flash-pivot move by a Baseliner up the lane. He can get a turnaround shot, or if challenged by the goalie he can dump to the Baseliner, who has remained at his low spot (Figure 5-12).

When playing against the T (Figure 3-7 in Chapter 3) the mid-defenders normally will be on top of the Shoulders when they drop back to the baseline, but when the Baseliners counter this by moving up the lane for the Cork's pass, the defense is forced to readjust. What will the goalie do? If he remains in front of the basket in line with the wings who are guarding the Shoulders, either of the Baseliners coming up will be open for the Cork's pass, and the subsequent shot from the free throw area. If the goalie moves out on defense, he still has to try to stop two men in the middle area. If he stays back and the wings move out when the Baseliners do, the Shoulders out wide on the baseline become potential scorers against him.

The normal Curl usually will not work against the 2-2-1 because the mid-defenders will pick up the Baseliners coming out over the picks of the Shoulders; however,

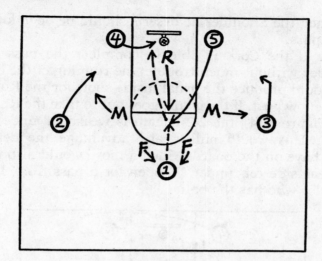

Figure 5-12

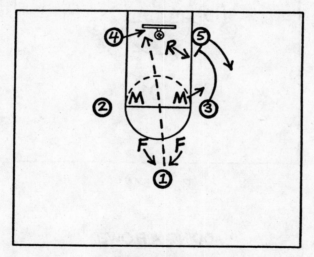

Figure 5-13

a Curl done by only one Shoulder can produce the alley-oop basket if the Cork and a Baseliner work well together (Figure 5-13). If the mid-defender drops back to stop the

Baseliner, the Shoulder he deserts should be open for the Cork's pass.

If the Cork is able to complete the pass to a Shoulder without much trouble, the running of the basic Jug should produce the usual inside shots for the Runner and the low post. If the goalie goes out to take the Runner (4 in Figure 5-14), the 2-2-1 team is weakened under the basket. This would nullify any advantage the defense might have on the boards. Such a move would also leave the weak-side rebounder (2) open for a pass from 3, the Shoulder who has the ball.

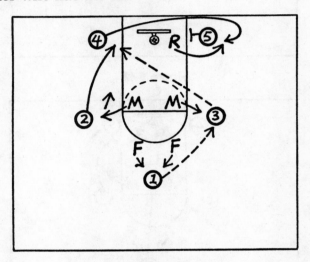

Figure 5-14

ADDING A FLOWER

It is worthwhile to use a flower against any zone in order to camouflage the Jug or to force the defense to change. Against the even-front zones, certain flowers are more valuable because they combat the double pressure so often put on the Cork by the two front-line defenders.

There are flowers that specifically help the Cork when he has the ball. Against the two outside ball handlers in the Jug's Two Cork set, the front-liners must split their defensive assignment, thus weakening the harassing strength usually applied to the ball in the hands of a single Cork. Setting up in a 1-3-1 or 1-4 alignment increases the number of the Cork's close potential receivers, and he needn't depend on just the Shoulders to relieve the pressure on him. These two sets are good to use when the defensive pressure is primarily aimed at preventing the Shoulders from receiving the ball, as often happens in the 2-3 or 2-2-1 zones.

Although the flowers enhance the offense, a team should not rely exclusively on them to make the Cork–Shoulder pass successful. The simple modifications to the basic Jug—the Shoulder High Post, the Shoulder Flex variations, the Shoulder Release and the Shoulder pick for the Cork—may be enough to do that job, and the flowers may be saved for other purposes.

When the two-man front defenses do not put much pressure on the Cork–Shoulders pass, other flower options may be used effectively. The Triple Stack (Figure 4-11 in Chapter 4) makes the 2-1-2 adjust if it hopes to stop the popper from taking his shot; L or R (Figure 4-1 in Chapter 4) forces the defense to shift to the loaded side immediately in order to stop the threat from that side; a Half Bean Pot (Figure 4-8 in Chapter 4), hurts the middle and back lines of all even-front zones that don't shift; the Double Stack (Figure 4-9 in Chapter 4) poses special problems for the 2-3 if its back line stays inside the stackers; and the open spots in all two-man front zones are exploited by the 1-3-1 formation.

6

BEATING THE ODD-FRONT ZONES

In general, the Jug operates against the odd-front zones in the same manner as it does against the even; however, there are some differences. The Cork is usually guarded directly by the top man in the zone, and he frequently is double-teamed when he ventures into the wing areas. More pressure is put on the Shoulders as the defense fights the Cork–Shoulder pass, and the Baseliners may be trapped in the corners more often than they are when working against the even fronts.

CORK ACTION

The 3-2 zone formation enhances the two-timing action against the Cork when he has the ball; and the 1-3-1 zone can easily make an upward shift of a wing to double-team the Cork. Whether doubled or not, the Cork, facing these or any other odd-front zones, can figure he'll meet at least one defensive man face to face—the one playing the point spot on defense.

The Cork follows the principle of attacking the pockets between defenders by going at the gaps between the defensive point and the wing defenders. This takes the point man to one side and at the same time tests the defensive players nearest the ball. If the wing on the ball side commits himself on the ball, then the Shoulder on that side may be open for receiving the Cork's pass. If the wing does not commit himself, the Cork may be able to penetrate to a good shooting spot. This occurs more often when the opponents play area-type zone defenses.

If the Cork does take the ball beyond, past the defending point, he will find that the 1-3-1 zone is stacked strongly in the middle and the 1-2-2 zone is usually adjusted to stopping play in that area; but against the 3-2 he may be able to exploit the weakness found in the middle.

SHOULDER ACTION

The Shoulders will find themselves matched up by the defense when normal Jug spots are taken against the 1-3-1 or the 1-2-2 zones. Against the former the middle is usually shut off in the beginning of the Jug action. Against both of these zones the Shoulders must be active in attempting to get free for the Cork's pass. After receiving the pass, the Shoulder will find most times that he can't get off the quick shot he may have obtained against the 2-1-2 or 2-3 zones. Normally there is a defensive wing in direct contact with him in the odd-front zones.

BASELINER ACTION

Against odd-front zones, the Baseliners face a situation similar to that posed by all zones. A Baseliner's position is really two passes away from the Cork, yet he may be able to get free for a skip pass from the Cork, depending on the type of zone and the ability of the defensive personnel. Against the 1-3-1 the Baseliners' out-numbering of the back-line defense can be used to advantage whenever the Cork has the ball or as soon as the Shoulder receives the Cork's pass.

The Baseliners should be wary of traps being sprung on them when they receive the ball out on the baseline—especially against the 3-2, in which a quick shift by a wing can put two defensive men on the ball in a hurry. Some 3-2s and some 1-3-1s will trap in the corners automatically every time the ball goes in there. The entire Jugging team should anticipate this trap.

ATTACKING THE 1-3-1

The Cork with the ball probes the area to either side of an imaginary mid-line bisecting the front court in an attempt to penetrate into the seam between the point guard and the defensive wing. He should not hold high hopes of getting free in the middle area, but if the defense plays it straight—point guard staying with the ball and getting no help from his wing or his middle man—a Cork with a height or jumping advantage over the point may be able to get a jump shot within his shooting range.

In the process of probing by the Cork, if the defensive wing releases from the Shoulder to help contain the Cork, the Shoulder can usually get open for the pass from the Cork. The Shoulder may be able to take his shot before the rest of the defense adjusts to the pass. If the Shoulder is picked up by the middle defender (M in Figure 6-1) covering for the wing (W)—who released to help against the Cork (1)—the passing lanes to the Baseliners or to the opposite Shoulder (2) may be open.

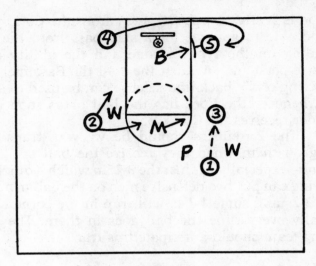

Figure 6-1

The opposite Shoulder (2) must read the defense. If the wing on this side drops into the middle, he slides down to his normal weak-side rebound spot; but if the wing drops back to defend in front of the basket, the Shoulder flashes into the free throw area (Figure 6-2). Note the path of 3 after his pass to the flasher (2). This move gives offensive rebounding balance and opens another passing option for the flasher, or for the Cork if the ball is cleared out to him.

The initial Jug positions taken by the Shoulders against the 1-3-1 tend to draw in the defensive wings. If they don't close in and the middle defender shifts to guard one Shoulder, the other Shoulder should be open either at his spot or after a quick move into the top of the key.

The Shoulders may be flanked with wing men on their outside. In this case the wings usually pressure toward the middle in defending against the Cork's pass. The middle defender attempts to stay balanced between the Shoulders and plays the ball as it is moved by the Cork, going to the ball when it comes in to the Shoulder. A slight spread by the Shoulders makes the middle de-

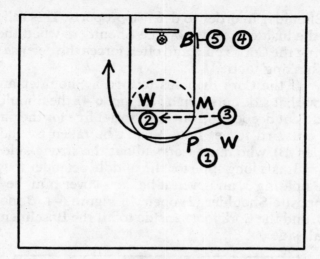

Figure 6-2

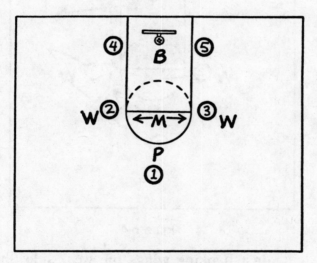

Figure 6-3

fender's job more difficult, especially if the Cork established himself in line with the basket (Figure 6-3). The
middle defender has to stay in a spot equidistant from

each Shoulder in order to defense properly. This relieves a bit of the inside pressure on the Shoulders when they are receiving the Cork's pass and often forces the defense out of their flanking tactic.

If the Cork dribbles toward a Shoulder and the wing on that side cuts him off (Figure 6-4), the Shoulder (3) should float deeper and outward to get free for the pass. By going outward to get free, 3 can't be taken by the back defender (B), who must worry about the strong-side Baseliner (5). It is a long slide for the middle defender to get out on the floating 3, and even if he does cover him, he leaves the opposite Shoulder (2) open. In Figure 6-4, B moves to take 3, and the Cork looks inside to hit the Baseliner (5) on the ball side.

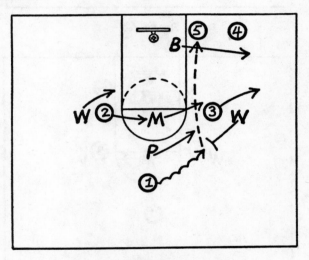

Figure 6-4

Against flanking wings the weak-side Shoulder, during normal Jug action, should attempt to keep his wing on his back as he goes down to rebound at his low off-side spot. In this manner he obtains a good rebound position inside the defensive man, and during his slide down the lane he may get open for a pass from the Cork or the Shoulder on the strong side.

If the 1-3-1 is played with the wings up in front of the Shoulders, it is very difficult for the Cork to hit the Shoulders in their original spots. The Shoulders have to fade outward to free themselves for a lob pass from the Cork. This move is similar to that made when the wing picks up the dribbling Cork. By fading, the Shoulders put more pressure on the middle defender and the back defender. If the back defender moves up to assist the middle defender in guarding a Shoulder, the Baseliner becomes open for the long skip-pass from the Cork.

A simple, effective move against wings who are fronting is the actual blocking of the wings by the Shoulders (Figure 6-5), which prevents them from covering the Baseliners, who widen out to get free for a pass from the Cork. The back defender cannot cover both widened Baseliners.

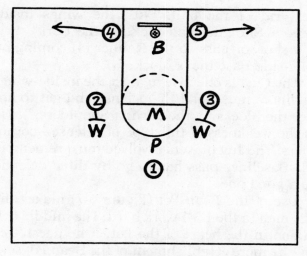

Figure 6-5

A tight 1-3-1 (Figure 6-6) played with the wings inside the Shoulders is another type of zone the Jug may face. The Jug formation itself nullifies the effectiveness of the middle defender (M), who is virtually wasted on defense. He has no real effect defensively until after the

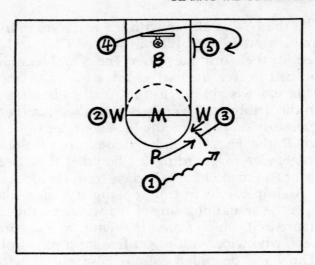

Figure 6-6

Cork gets rid of the ball. With the wings inside the Shoulders, a Shoulder can pick for the Cork, springing him for a shot, or pass to the Runner (4) coming around the strong-side Baseliner's block.

The Curl is effective against the inside-wing 1-3-1. The Baseliners must read the defense and get to an open spot after the blocks by the curling Shoulders. This move exploits the weakness of this type of defense—coverage of the corners. The Jug players involved must remember that the Cork–Baseliner pass has to go by three defenders; it must be a good one.

Use of the Bean Pot (Figure 6-7) makes the four "outside" men in the 1-3-1 work hard. The middle defender is left alone in the heart of the Pot. If he doesn't change position, the mere establishment of the Bean Pot set opens up shot opportunities as the ball is moved around the periphery.

The creases between the middle defender and the wings are filled by either or both Baseliners flashing straight up the lane. This puts the middle defender in a tenuous position. He can't stop the pass unless he has help from a wing. If a wing makes a move inside to help, the Shoulder on that side will be open.

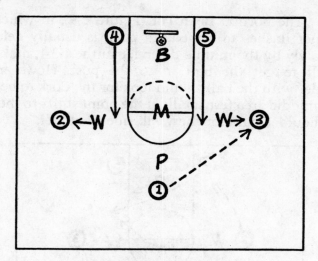

Figure 6-7

If, in combatting the Bean Pot, the back defender moves up to fill in for the middle defender who covers a flashing Baseliner, the Shoulders should make back-door cuts (Figure 6-8). The Cork passes to one of the Flashers, as 2 and 3 go back-door.

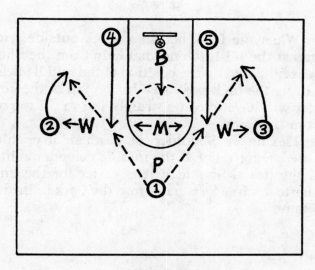

Figure 6-8

The normal Bean Pot (Figure 6-9), in which the Baseliner flashes to a medium post, is usually defensed adequately by the middle defender in the 1-3-1, making it difficult to get the ball in to the post. However, the Shoulder with the ball should look for the Cork to be open in the middle area (especially if the point shifts to the ball-side Shoulder) and for the weak-side Shoulder.

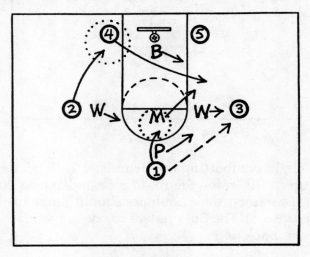

Figure 6-9

When the Cork becomes stuck outside with the ball against the 1-3-1, the normal help from the Shoulder Release is hindered by the position of the middle defender, who patrols the high-post area in the top of the key. The Shoulder will have to come straight out to get the release pass from the Cork.

Flexing one Shoulder can be an aid in opening the top of the key for relief. If the middle defender shifts over toward the flexed Shoulder, it is easier for the unflexed Shoulder to get free for a pass from the Cork in the middle area (Figure 6-10).

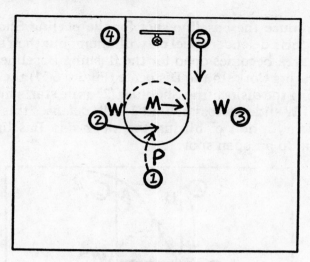

Figure 6-10

ATTACKING THE 1-2-2

This zone actually matches the set of the Jug. In some ways each Jugger can figure that he is being guarded by one man. The Cork is not defensed by more than one man until he ventures near the Shoulder area. The Shoulders are going one on one with their defensive men when the ball is at the Cork. Usually the defenders play inside the Shoulders, so the Shoulders normally shake free to the outside. Another move for them is to go over the top of their defensive men to get free for the Cork's pass.

Whenever the Shoulders move outward, thus drawing out the defense, a Baseliner may be able to flash in front of the hoop for a direct hit from the Cork.

Most of the Jug options can be effective against the 1-2-2, but the Curl will be the least successful due to the simple adjustment that the defense can make. The T will produce the baseline shot for the peeling Shoulders unless their defenders peel off with them; but then the free throw area becomes open for the flashing Baseliners or a penetrating Cork. In the Dislocate (Figure 6-11) the option of hitting the dislocating Shoulder (2) as he starts his cut is there if W slides across behind 2. If W defenses this way, it opens the option of hitting the weak-side Baseliner (4) flashing to an open spot.

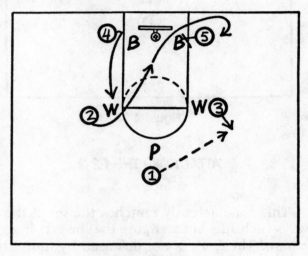

Figure 6-11

The Bean Pot opens up the middle area even more if the defenders go out on the Shoulders. A penetrating Cork can be used to good advantage here, and there is more room for the flashing off-side Baseliner than he finds against zones where the middle is clogged by the defense.

Due to the matching offense–defense alignment of players, the flowers will produce good shots after the normal Jug has been set up and run. A quick change of the set into L, R, the 1-3-1, or the 1-4, will shake up the 1-2-2.

ATTACKING THE 3-2

Although the 3-2 can be Jugged in much the same manner as the 1-2-2, there are some aspects of the 3-2 that are unique and should be considered. Usually the wings will play ahead of the Shoulders, and they will strongly challenge the Cork–Shoulder pass by cutting off the passing lanes. The Shoulders may use the open top of the key area to spring free for passes from the Cork. The skip pass from Cork to Runner, whether he is the Baseliner or the dislocated Shoulder (Figure 6-12), is a natural against the 3-2.

The Bean Pot spreads the defensive wings and allows the Baseliners to pop into the open middle area to receive the Cork's pass.

Against the 3-2 the Cork must be wary of being two-timed by the defensive point and a wing; the Shoulders must be ready to help in case of the Cork trap.

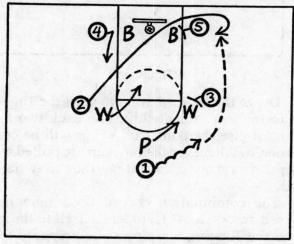

Figure 6-12

Often a team will use the 3-2 because it has only two big men and wishes to use them to the best advantage. The Jug can pressure this type of team. The normal shift of the defensive back line (Figure 6-13), the big players, to cover the Baseline Runner leaves the defense at a disadvantage in rebounding on the weak side, where their small wing man (W) is matched up with the Jug's Shoulder or Baseliner (4) in case the Dislocate move is made.

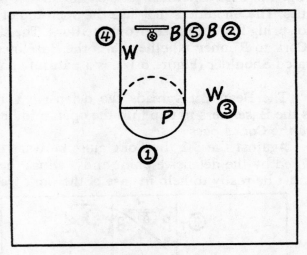

Figure 6-13

Use of the 1-4 formation to start the Jug will force the 3-2 to make a radical shift. The back two men must move out, or else the point and wings will be completely outnumbered. Whenever the big men are pulled away from the hoop, any rebound advantage they may have had is lessened.

The combination of two good rebounders and three speedsters on a 3-2 team lends itself to the fast break game; so the Jugging team must be prepared to combat this. Rebounding, quick reaction to the transition game, and defensive balance are of paramount importance.

7

BEATING THE "SPECIAL" ZONES

Unorthodox or special defenses are used by many teams in order to apply their strengths, hide their weaknesses, confuse opponents, and neutralize the opponent's star or stars. Jugging teams should be prepared to meet these defenses: the Box-and-One, the Diamond-and-One, the Triangle-and-Two, the Match-Up, Alternating Zones, and Man-for-Man Mix with Zone. Usually, just running the normal Jug continuity against these special defenses is sufficient to create scoring opportunities; however, the Jugsters should be aware of specific options in the offense that may prove very effective against these combination defenses.

ATTACKING THE BOX-AND-ONE

Because of the configuration of the Jug set, most Box-and-One defenses operate against the Jug in the same fashion as does the Diamond-and-One. With one defensive player concentrating on a specific player and the other four defenders zoning, the normal Jug sequences present most of the problems they give the straight zones. The "star" may be slowed by the defense's special tactic of man-for-manning him, but if he realizes what is happening and does not allow himself to become frustrated, and if the balance of his team does not fret about the additional pressure on him, there is usually no reason to vary the operation of the Jug.

If the Cork is the player who is man-for-manned, the Shoulders should work hard to help him get free to make his pass or get a shot. The team can consider that they are attacking something similar to a 1-2-2 zone. The four zoning defenders invariably play as they would in a 1-2-2.

If the manned Cork goes through or trades spots with a Shoulder, the defense will have to be modified to accommodate this change, unless it is only the *position* (the Cork) and not the man that is being man-for-manned. In case of the man-for-manning of the spot itself, a switch of personnel from Cork to Shoulder will leave the Box-and-One in its 1-2-2 alignment and will be continued to be treated as that by the Jug. During the Pick-Roll reverse action (Figure 7-1) against the team manning the Cork, the Runner (4) on the strong side will be left open as the four zoners shift with the ball to the weak side. The defensive back (A), who is out on the Runner, must shift quickly to fill in for (B), who is defending under the basket and must pick up the roller. If C drops in to aid, the strong-side Shoulder (3) should flash to the free throw area. In a normal 1-2-2 the point would be covering there, but because the point is man-for-manning the Cork, who has the ball on the drive, that area is left open. Another option on the reversing of the ball from the strong side is the Cork back-dooring an overzealous man-for-manner who attempts to cut off the pass out to him.

In the type of Box-and-One described, the Cork gets treatment similar to that which he receives when

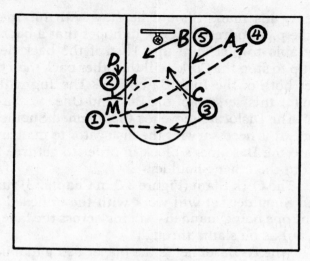

Figure 7-1

playing against most aggressive front lines in a 1-2-2, 3-2, or 1-3-1 zone. It is when he is double-teamed by a boxing player who is helping the manning defender that there is a difference, but even here it is not unlike any wing-trapping zone. As in all cases when the ball is two-timed, the offense outnumbers the defense somewhere on the court. This is what you should exploit when the Box-and-One doubles on the star.

The Shoulders must be active in relieving the pressure on the Cork when he is manned and/or double-teamed. Opening the Cork–Shoulder passing lanes by use of the 1-4 flower or the Bean Pot is also a help. If the box opens up with the spread of the offensive set, the Cork may be able to take his man to the basket.

When the Shoulder is the player man-for-manned in the Box-and-One, the box has to distort in order to contain the Cork. So the defense is forced to adjust immediately to the Jug formation. A pick for the driving Cork by the manned Shoulder creates a dilemma for the man-for-manner. Should he step out to stop the Cork and thus leave his man? Should he stay with his man and allow the pick to free the Cork in hopes that a back boxer will be able to pick him up? Then if the back defender moves up to stop the Cork, will the other back man be able to cover both of the Jug's Baseliners? The Jug will make trouble for this version of the Box-and-One.

The Dislocate move for the manned Shoulder is a good one. It is necessary for the dislocator to maneuver his man into the Baseliner's block in order to get free for the pass from the other Shoulder.

The Cork Slant (Figure 3-3 in Chapter 3) run off of a flexed Shoulder set will work with the unflexed Shoulder—the one being manned—slicing across the lane off the Cork's tail as he slants through.

When a Baseliner is the player being manned, the zone portion of the defense usually resembles a diamond with one man defending in front of the basket, two wing men up near the Shoulders, and a man on top near the Cork. The manned Baseliner on the Baseline run must finesse his man so that he runs him into the block by the other Baseliner; or if he is defensed on the baseline side when he starts the run, he should come up over the top of the Blocker.

The Curl (Figure 3-8 in Chapter 3) is effective in springing the Baseliner being manned. The head-hunting Shoulder attempting to pin down the opponent manning the Baseliner should pivot back so that he is facing the ball after his screen. Frequently he is left open because the back man on the diamond becomes concerned with defensing on the other side of the court where the other Shoulder has come down to screen him. If the back diamond man plays strong on the side of the manned Baseliner, you should expect the low Shoulder on the other side of the court to be open.

In case you have a team that seems to run a certain part of the Jug offense better than others, use that phase of the Jug, and place the manned player in the spot where he can be most effective or in one that makes the rest of the team more effective. Don't forget to substitute for the player being manned. Often a short rest will help him, and sometimes pulling him out of the game serves to confuse the defense when they adjust their manning action to a new player.

ATTACKING THE DIAMOND-AND-ONE

When the Cork is manned, a true diamond defensive formation by the four zoners allows the Shoulders of the Jug much freedom; so normally the diamond distorts into a box. As such, it is Jugged as if you were facing a Box-and-One. Similarly when either a Shoulder or a Baseliner is manned, the positions of the zoning players resembles the Box-and-One so much that the same type of Jug action that was successful against that defense may be used effectively against the Diamond-and-One.

ATTACKING THE TRIANGLE-AND-TWO

This defense, which usually attempts to keep three big defenders near the basket while two man-for-manners work the outside, should not produce problems for the Jugging team. The men underneath will be blocked and positioned just as they are when you are Jugging against ordinary zones. The triangle can be treated in the same way as the middle and back men in the 2-1-2 zone. The two other defenders have to make decisions. One, probably, will take the Cork, and the other will pick up one of the Shoulders.

A pick for the Cork angling in, if done by the Shoulder being manned, may cause a switch in defensive assignments by the two defenders. This is the same adjustment that has to be made against this maneuver by a common zone. A pick on the other side of the court by the Shoulder not being manned (Figure 7-2) causes the middle Zoner (M) to help against the Cork. At that time the Shoulder (3) may become free. If the back defender steps up to help against 3, a Baseliner becomes uncovered; so the situation reverts to pure basketball—can the offense beat the defense to open spots and get the ball there?

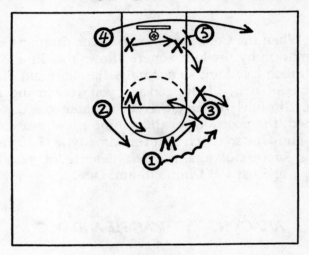

Figure 7-2

The Cork's pass to the manned Shoulder means that the triangle has to adjust as it would in a 2-1-2. If the back defender on the ball side slides out on the Runner, either the middle man must drop down or the other back man must come up to cover the off-side Shoulder (Figure 7-3), who will be free due to man-for-man commitments on the Cork and the ball-side Shoulder. A sag by the man guarding the Cork leaves open the opportunity for the Cork to get the ball back from the Shoulder and be in closer to the basket.

When the Jug continuity reaches the point where the weak-side Pick-Roll action is taking place, with the manned Cork and the manned Shoulder down low work-

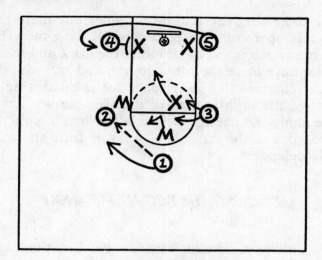

Figure 7-3

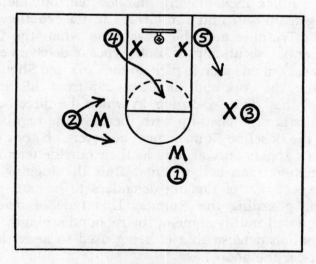

Figure 7-4

ing together, who is going to pick up the new Cork outside? Will one of the triangle men come out that far? Can the player manning the picker follow him on his roll and fight through the double screen on the loaded side of the court?

The Bean Pot can cause problems for the triangle (Figure 7-4). Who goes out wide to guard the unmanned

Shoulder? Moving the middle defender out there leaves the middle open for a lot of basketball. Low men (Baseliners) may flash up to the middle; the Cork and manned Shoulder have more room to operate; and even the zoned Shoulder can use the open space for maneuvering. The removal of the middle man of the triangle weakens the defense along the baseline, especially when 5 is the Runner and goes to the far side of 4 (away from the middle triangle defender).

ATTACKING THE TWO-AND-TRIANGLE

This man-for-man and zone combination capitalizes on the strength of two big men under the basket and/or three quick men playing man-for-man outside. Your Jugging team will find similarities in the reactions of a Two-and-Triangle and the 1-2-2 zone when the Cork–Shoulder pass is attempted. Both types of defenses expect their three outside men to pick up the Cork and Shoulders. Therefore, the Cork and Shoulders can treat this defense much as they do a 1-2-2 zone, in which the three outside defenders are matched up with them. In the regular Jug action the Baseline Runner must be covered by one of the two back zoners only as long as their outside teammates have man-for-man assignments. Thus the Jugging team may expect one of the big defenders to be out on the baseline guarding the Runner. This type of defensive coverage will nullify some of the rebound strength of the combination defense that is being used to keep the big men under the hoop.

The middle is vulnerable in this defense. If the manning defenders stay with their men at the Shoulder and Cork spots and the big men "park" under the basket area, the middle is left open for the Baseliners to flash through. The Bean Pot will work well against the defense.

The open center allows flashing movement by the Base-liners as well as the possibility of back-door cuts by the Shoulders when a flashing Baseliner receives the Cork's pass in the top of the free-throw circle.

In the Dislocate the slanting Shoulder attempts to brush off his defensive man on the blocking Baseliner in the same manner as in most man-for-man offensive brush-ing moves. The Blocker's action is the same as that used against any regular zone defense.

ATTACKING THE MATCH-UP ZONE

Matching up with the Jug puts the defense into a 1-2-2 alignment. The Jugging team should attack it as if it were a 1-2-2 zone. The defense will shift and distort as the offense progresses, and there is no need to make special adjustments. Weaknesses in the defense will appear as the Jug probes into it. Regardless of the Match-Up, if the defense is a zone, certain shifts and adjustments that occur in normal zones must occur, and these are the things the Jug is built to combat.

The special Match-Up zones (sometimes called "Rule Defense"), in which a cerain player follows his match-up's cut and then later releases his man to a zoning teammate, presents no unique problems for the Jug. In the Cork Slant (Figure 7-5) X1 may follow 1 all the way to the baseline, in which case he can't release 1 to X5 because X5 must work with X4 to defense the baseline run action on the other side of the lane. If X1 does release 1 to X5 and then returns to his frontal duties, 4 and 5 outnumber X4 on the strong side. If X1 follows a rule of staying with his match-up one or two steps into the 3-second lane (a popular method of defense) and then releases 1 to X3 (Figure 7-6), 3 becomes open. If X1 defenses 3, 3's move is to dislocate (Figure 7-7), and 1 will either return to the Cork

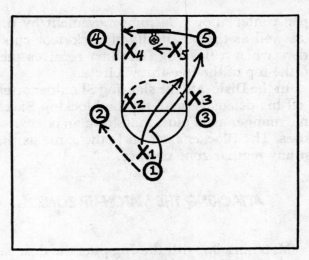

Figure 7-5

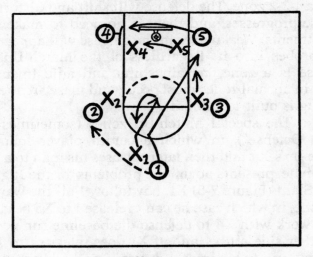

Figure 7-6

spot or take the off-side rebounding spot as 5 rotates to the Cork spot.

In Cork Through (Figure 7-8) X1 will have difficulty releasing 1 to X2 because X2 is busy defending 2, who has the ball. If X1 releases 1 to X4, 4 will be left open near

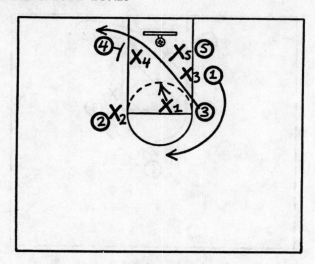

Figure 7-7

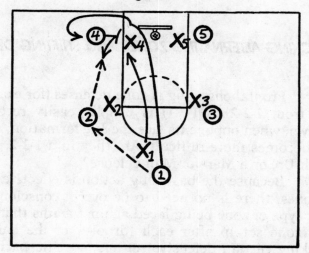

Figure 7-8

the basket. If X1 picks up 4, there may be a mismatch in size, and 4 should be given the ball for a power move.

In the Dislocate (Figure 7-9) X2 may follow 2 across the lane and release him to X5. In this case 5 merely blocks X5 as he would against any normal zone defense.

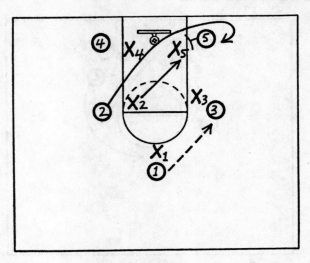

Figure 7-9

ATTACKING ALTERNATING ZONES AND SHIFTING DEFENSES

Frontal changing of zone defenses (for example, a shift from 1-2-2 to 1-3-1) is usually easily recognized; however, when opponents face the Jug formation, recognition becomes more difficult. Are they in a 1-2-2, a 3-2, a Match-Up, or a Man-for-Man defense?

Because the basic Jug action is effective against all zones, there is no need to be overly conscious of the exact type of zone being faced against teams that change their zone set-up after each turnover of the ball. If, in attacking certain defensive set-ups, specific parts of the Jug continuity or specific offensive sets are more effective, it is prudent to repeat what has been most successful.

The mixed defense of alternating Man-for-Man with Zone regularly throughout the game or on a planned schedule throughout the game should not prove bothersome to your Jugging team. An easy test for man-for-man occurs during the baseline run action. Observe what happens when the Runner goes around the block. An automatic switch by man-for-manners there might be confusing, but running a Dislocate should clear things up. If the defensive man on the Shoulder follows him through on his diagonal cut around the block, it probably is man-for-man, or it could be a Match-Up. A switch, in which the man guarding the Blocker goes out on the Shoulder Runner and the Shoulder's defensive man picks up the Blocker, is easy to detect. This switch is not very common because often it will leave a smaller man guarding the low-posting Blocker, which is, of course, an advantage for the offensive team.

If you have prepared your team to run their offense effectively and have explained that most of the combination defenses are gimmicks used as a last resort to upset the team, the team should be able to attack with confidence.

Because so much of the Jug action is effective against man-for-man tactics, it is possible to continue Jugging as an opponent switches from zone to man-for-man and obtain scoring opportunities against either type of defense. The Pick-Roll reverse action, the blocking and screening play, the back-door action, and the one-on-one play of the Jug are all sound ways of beating man-for-man.

8

AUXILIARY JUG PLAY

FAST BREAKING WITH THE JUG

The Jug is easily incorporated into your team's fast break. A Jugging team can swing into its offense immediately if the primary phase of the fast break has not produced a percentage shot.

If in the normal break with the traditional filling of lanes it is apparent that a good shot is not obtainable, a Jug continuity may be used. With the ball in the middle and the wings cutting to the hoop, one wing continues across the lane and around the other wing's block just as the Runner does around the Baseliner's in the Jug. The middle man with the ball becomes the Shoulder with normal Jug options: pass to either Baseliner or to the off-side low man—the trailer in the break, who is following the rule of exploding through the weak side. The last man up the court on the break takes the Cork position.

There is a variety of ways to designate which side of the court to run the Jug as the secondary phase of the break. It can be done on an automatic basis of always going to a specified side of the court. If it is to be run on the left side, the middle breaker (M) with the ball (Figure 8-1) looks to that side and may even veer to the left side for

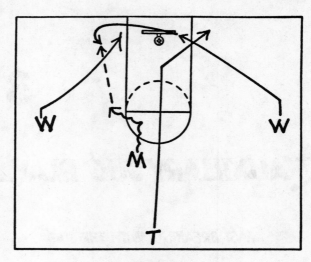

Figure 8-1

better passing angles. The right wing (W) continues on through after his angled cut to the basket and goes around the block by the left wing (W), who has stopped after his cut. The trailer (T) goes in low on the right side of the basket, and the fifth man up court takes over at the Cork spot as the Jug action starts.

Another means of designating the side for Jugging is to key on the position of the middle man as he approaches the free throw area. He may veer to one side as he reaches the top of the key, thus indicating the side for Jugging if no shot is obtained from the break itself. The wings will react to this move and set up their part of the Jug as needed.

Still another way to Jug after the break is to have the trailer (fourth man up court) become the Runner. In this case both wings, after their cuts to the basket, establish themselves as blockers for the trailer. The trailer, after going through, goes around one of the blocking wings and looks for the pass from the middle man (now the Shoulder).

If your wings tend to decelerate too early on their cut to the basket in order to block, you may wish to change their assignments and have them go hard to the hoop and cross under the basket to establish their blocks on the opposite side of the basket (Figure 8-2). This gives them ample time to slow down for their blocks as they cross the lane under the basket. It also opens passing options to them before the trailer comes through, thus putting more pressure on the defense than was generated by the "stop-and-block-on-your-side" method.

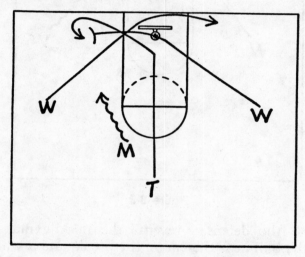

Figure 8-2

If the trailer is supposed to become the Runner, you must set some rules. Do you want the trailer always cutting to one side? Do you want to allow him the option of going either way? Do you want him to key on the position of the middle man with the ball?

Regardless of which method is used to run the Jug as the secondary phase of the break or which method is used to designate the side of the court to be overloaded, a slight variation occurs if a wing has possession of the ball

in the front court. If in the final action of the break a pass
to a wing has failed to produce a shot, the ball should go
back to the middle man to start the Jug action. If a wing
drives and then has to pull up near the basket, he can
reverse pivot and feed the other wing, who has come across
as the Runner (Figure 8-3). The Jug is on!

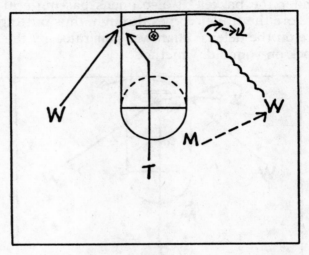

Figure 8-3

   If the defense prevents the middle man from
having the ball near the end of the break, and a wing has
possession, the middle man cuts to the hoop and, if he is
not hit by the wing, blocks for the other wing, who
becomes the Runner.

   A Jugging team need not learn a new offense as a
secondary phase of its break because it already has the
offense in its arsenal. Because the fast break is one very
effective way of beating zones, the Jugging team should
consider using it; also, it lends itself so well to the basic
Jug offense. Another point in favor of Jugging is that the
Jug, as a secondary phase of the break, is effective against
man-for-man defense because of its organization for the
transition game. The Baseliner block for the Runner, the

Pick-Roll reverse action, and the use of the double screen after the roll are all solid anti-man-for-man tactics.

JUGGING HALF-COURT TRAPS

The word "carboy," which in reality is the name of a large jug, is used to refer to the Jug trap breaker. The Jugging team only has to expand its basic set into a larger Jug to go into this method of beating the trap. The Baseliners move up the lane halfway between the brick and the free throw line and three feet out from the lane line. The Shoulders get in line with the Baseliners on spots three feet ahead of the top of the free throw circle (Figure 8-4).

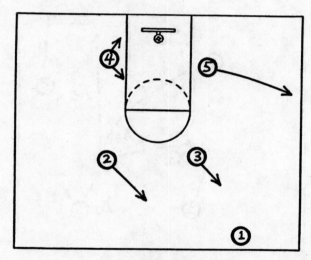

Figure 8-4

All players key to the Cork. Usually the defense springs its trap on the ball just after it is brought across the 10-second line. The Cork, who knows he will be facing the trap, usually selects a side of the front court to enter, or if he crosses the line in the center of the court, he heads to one side immediately. Entry of the ball into one side of the front court triggers the moves of the Juggers.

The ball-side Shoulder (3) breaks out directly to an open spot, looking for the ball. The other Shoulder stays on his side of the front court, coming out enough to give the Cork a favorable passing angle to him. The ball-side Baseliner (5) breaks out on an angle to the sideline. Now, the about-to-be-trapped Cork has four passing options: (1) the longest, to the off-side Baseliner (4), who remains in his original area; (2) the riskiest, across court to 2; (3) to 5 on the sideline; and (4) the short pass to 3.

The pass to 3 is the preferred option (Figure 8-5) because it gets the ball past the trappers and puts the offense in a dominant position. The defense is now outnumbered up front, and the offense should move immediately to take advantage of the situation.

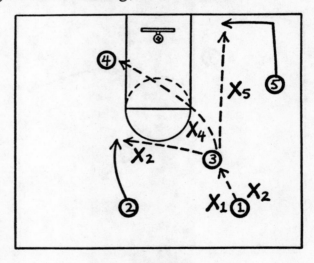

Figure 8-5

There are several options for 3 (Figure 8-5). A ridiculously easy basket is obtained if a pass is made to the Baseliner (4). Surprisingly, this simple option is often effective against trapping teams. Players 5 and 2, being one pass away from 3, usually cause the defense to play as diagrammed. Players X2 and X5 are anticipating stealing the pass from the trapped Cork. It is apparent that there is a defensive weakness along the line from 1 to 3 to 4. Player X4 has to try to contain both 3 and 4. If X4 hangs back on 4, then 3, on receiving the ball, drives to the hoop. If the drive draws in X5 and/or X2, 3 looks for 5 boxing in from the corner or 2 cutting to the open weak-side area.

If the Cork can't pass to 3 and, instead, passes to 5, 3 cuts down the lane looking for the ball (Figure 8-6). If he doesn't receive it, he blocks low for the baseline Runner (4) coming across in typical Jug fashion, and 2 takes the off-side rebounding spot. If no shot is obtained, and trapping continues after each pass, quick movement of the ball into one of the reverse-action patterns should produce a good shot.

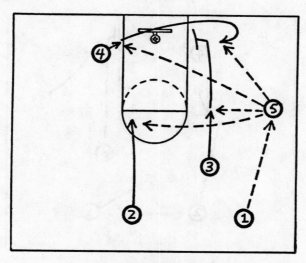

Figure 8-6

On receiving the ball, 5 looks to hit 3 on his cut. He also should look to 4, who may have been open but not seen by the trapped Cork and may still be open; or he may have become open after the 1-to-5 pass. There is also the possibility that 2 will be open as he fills in for 4, running the baseline.

The pass from Cork to 2 is a dangerous one. A steal by the defense here normally results in a lay-in at the other end of the court. Sometimes, however, it may be a necessity pass. We cannot place too much emphasis on the need for 2 to *meet* the pass.

There must be a strong move to the ball, and there can be no lobbing of the ball. Proper passing and receiving techniques are necessary to prevent a steal of the ball.

If 2 receives the ball, he may find 4 open inside, or with 4 he may exploit the situation on that side of the court (Figure 8-7). Even with the defense balanced, the Pick-Roll can be run with 5 and 3 preparing for the double screen if the roller needs it. Player 1 moves over to the ball side for the possible relay pass.

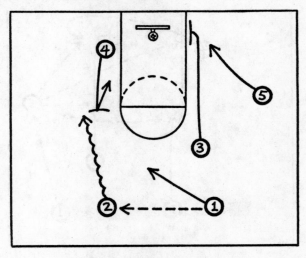

Figure 8-7

The long pass from Cork to low Baseliner (4) will go if the defense pulls out to trap. Here is where the tall player at the Cork spot is effective. He can see over the defense better and can pass over trappers more easily than a short Cork. The lob pass is dangerous—trapping teams love it—so emphasis must be put on getting off high, crisp passes to get by the trappers and their secondary line of defense.

During all the action near mid-court 4 should not park; rather, he should move about in order to get open for a pass. If he does receive the ball directly from 1 or 3 and is not able to shoot, 4 may look at 5 across the lane, 2 on his side of the court, and 3 coming down the gut (Figure 8-8).

If the Carboy does not produce a shot and the trap is called off, the Jug should be set up with players taking the spot closest to them. Usually these will be the same relative spots they had when first positioning for the Carboy.

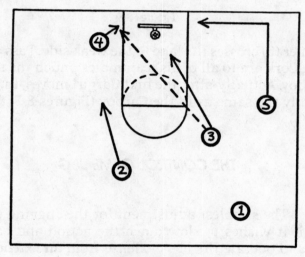

Figure 8-8

A variation of the Carboy, called "Cargirl," starts from the expanded Jug set, with different moves for the players. As the trap is being sprung on the Cork (Figure 8-9), the near Shoulder (3) sprints to the sideline; the far Shoulder (2) moves out closer to the Cork; and the far Baseliner (4) breaks out to the top of the key. The near

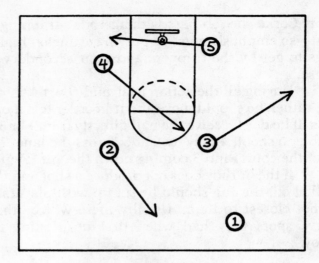

Figure 8-9

Baseliner (5) crosses the lane to the weak side. Pass options for the Cork are to all of his teammates, much the same as in Carboy. Actually, after the first Cargirl moves, the action is exactly the same as in the Carboy (Figures 8-5, 8-6, 8-7, and 8-8).

THE CONTROL GAME JUG

The simplest adjustment for the Jugging team to make if it wishes to slow down the action and consume time is to operate the basic offense from an extended set. The more open set makes passing easier because all players concentrate on getting free to receive a pass rather than getting free to score. When the defense starts to concentrate mainly on preventing passes and stealing the ball, the offense should take advantage of the overplay and go to the basket.

No matter which set or flower is used to start the control game, the offensive players must concentrate on getting free to receive passes. For the normal Jug the Carboy set may be employed. The Shoulders have more room to receive the Cork's pass; the Baseline runner can go farther out along the baseline looking for the ball; and the Cork can float out farther, waiting for clear-out passes and the reversal of the ball.

If the defense does not expand to fight the extended Jug formation, the outside three—Cork and both Shoulders—can "play catch" to consume time. When the defense does come out, a move outward by the Shoulders sets up a wide Bean Pot (Figure 8-10) and opens up the middle for penetration regardless of whether the defense is an odd front zone, as diagrammed, or an even front. The usual options of the Bean Pot may be used from this expanded formation.

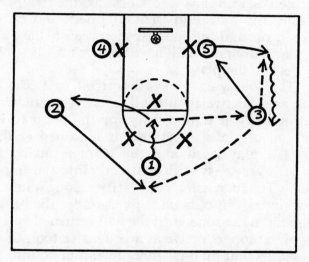

Figure 8-10

Simple moves by the Jug's outer three players can also help to "eat up the clock." With the defense spread, the Cork may attempt to drive the middle. Once stopped, he dishes off to one Shoulder and then goes away from the pass to fill in for the other Shoulder, who has come out to replace the Cork (Figure 8-10). In case the Shoulder has trouble returning the ball out to the Cork spot, he can pass to the Baseliner on his side, who moves out along the baseline to help. After his pass, the Shoulder cuts down to the Baseliner spot as the original Baseliner (5) dribbles out to a wide Shoulder spot. This type of action, inside and outside movement, causes the defense to contract and expand.

BASELINE OUT-OF-BOUNDS PLAYS

A modification of the Jug formation can be used to run out-of-bounds plays under the basket. The least complicated set-up has the Cork as the trigger man, inbounding the ball, and the Baseliners and Shoulders taking their normal Jug spots. If you prefer to have another player inbounding the ball, have the Cork trade spots with that player for the play.

The following plays, described as Series A and Series B, are effective against all defenses, including man-for-man, making it unnecessary for the team to learn a different set of plays. If no shot is obtained at the conclusion of a play itself and the team is facing a zone defense, it is very easy to flow directly into the Jug offense continuity. The increasing popularity among man-for-man teams of zoning out-of-bounds plays under the basket and then staying in the zone until the ball is turned over makes the Jug even more effective as an offensive tool. Of course, against teams that man-for-man the out-of-bounds play or resort to their man defense after the play has been run, you may want to swing into your man-for-man offense if no shot results from the play.

Series A

On a signal from 1, both Baseliners run to the corners; the off-side Shoulder (2) streaks to the hoop; and the ball-side Shoulder (3) drops back (Figure 8-11). Player 1 has four possible receivers: either Baseliner in a corner, the off-side Shoulder (2), and his last resort, the ball-side Shoulder (3).

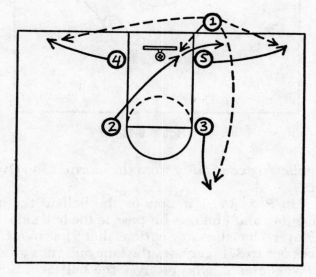

Figure 8-11

In *Play A-1*, Baseliner 5 receives the ball (Figure 8-12), looks inside for 2, and may take a shot himself—or if neither of his first two options is used, he clears out to 3. Meanwhile, 4 comes back to the lane. If 2 receives the ball from 5 and can't shoot, he clears the ball out to 3; 1 comes around 4's block as 3 dribbles hard to obtain a good passing angle to 2. If no shot is obtained from this action,

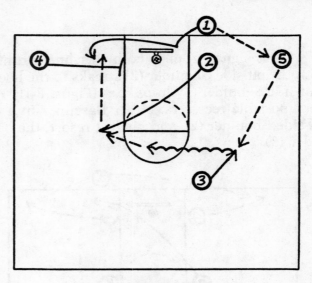

Figure 8-12

the regular Jug continuity from this normal Jug Overload is used.

In *Play A-2*, 1 in-bounds the ball to the off-side Baseliner (4), and 1 follows his pass to the ball side (Figure 8-13). Player 4 has the same options that 5 has in A-1. As the ball goes out to 3, 1 recrosses the lane and runs around 5's block. Whenever 2, who receives the ball at a Shoulder spot from 3, can't pass to the Runner (1) or the Blocker (5), he clears back out to 3, who goes directly into the reverse action on the weak side.

The in-bound pass from 1 to the off-side Shoulder (2) signals the start of *Play A-3*. This pass to 2 is only made when 2 has beaten the defense and is free for a shot. If he receives the in-bound pass and can't shoot, 2 fires the ball out to 5 or 2, and the play continues as in A-1. Similarly in *Play A-4*, 1 in-bounds to 3, who has dropped back to a release point, and the Jug action follows, with 1 going around 4's block and 2 coming back up to a Shoulder spot to relay the ball from 3 to 1 as in A-1.

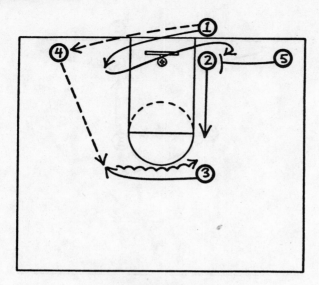

Figure 8-13

Late in a game, after Series A plays have been used several times, a slight change may surprise the defense. In *Play A-5* (Figure 8-14), 2 and 3 switch assignments. Player 3 fakes dropping back and then goes straight down the lane to the ball. Often, in cases where 3 has a height or jumping advantage, he can tip in a lobbed inbound pass from 1. Even without a height or jumping advantage, 3 often gets the tip-in opportunity merely from the surprise element of his new move. If 1 does not lob the ball to 3, the other options of Series A are used.

Other variations may be used to ease the pressure on the in-bound pass. In one variation, the ball-side Shoulder (3) cuts to the corner on his side of the court while the Baseliner (5) holds on that side. The off-side Shoulder (2) does not go to the ball but fades back to get free for the outlet pass. Another option calls for the off-side Shoulder (2) to go to the corner on his side while the off-side Baseliner (4) goes across the lane toward the trigger man.

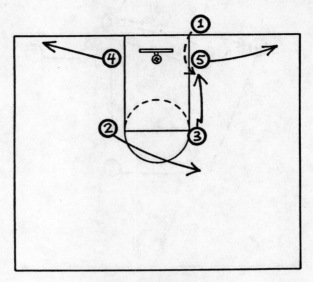

Figure 8-14

Series D (for Dislocate)

This version of the basic Jug baseline out-of-bounds action is based on the Dislocate move used in the

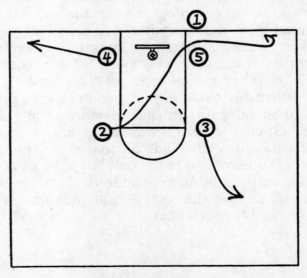

Figure 8-15

normal Jug. On the signal for D the off-side Shoulder (2 in Figure 8-15) goes to the ball and squeezes through between 5 and the defensive man guarding 1. Player 2 then goes out to the corner. The other three players make the same moves as those in Series A. Player 1 has the same passing options as in Series A.

If the Dislocate out-of-bounds play is run from the other side with 3 going past 4 and out to the off-side corner, 2 drops back. Player 4 crosses the lane after 3 goes by. The set-up of players' positions is now the same as in Series A.

SIDELINE OUT-OF-BOUNDS PLAY

Whenever the zone moves out to challenge the inbound pass from the sideline, the Jug turns on its side with the tallest or best-jumping player, 4, at the Shoulder spot (Figure 8-16). The other spots should be filled as closely as possible to the personnel alignment used in the normal Jug offense being used. The Shoulders screen laterally for

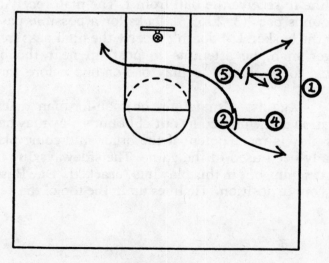

Figure 8-16

the Baseliners, who cut to the front and rear corners of the half court on the ball side. Player 4 goes hard to the basket, and 3 pivots after his screen and comes back to meet a possible pass from 1. Player 1 has four pass options. A pass to either corner is usually followed by setting up the normal Jug offense. A pass to 3 may result in an outnumbering of the defense under the basket as 5 breaks to the hoop and 4 comes to the ball. Player 1 passes to 4 only if he gets free.

MID-COURT OUT-OF-BOUNDS PLAY

With the ball out of bounds at the middle of the court, the Jug is set up sideways, with the 10-second line running down the center of the Jug (Figure 8-17). The Shoulders break outward toward the sideline while the Baseliner in the back court screens for his partner coming into the back court; 4 breaks to the hoop after screening for 5. Player 1 can nearly always count on being able to pass to 3 because the path of the ball is completely out of bounds and no opponent can legally position himself in that path. Player 3 should get to a point just inside the sideline to receive the ball from 1. The man receiving the in-bounds pass (3, 2, or 5), looks for a possible pass to 4 near the basket. If 4 doesn't receive the high pass from the trigger man, he attempts to post up near the basket, hoping for a chance to play one-on-one before the zone regroups.

Against a match-up or man-for-man defense, a variation of the mid-court out-of-bounds play may be used. This play is more potent if the other mid-court play has already been used in the game. The sideways Jug formation is set up, but in this play it is "cracked." One Baseliner, 5, is "out of position." He lines up in the top of the key area

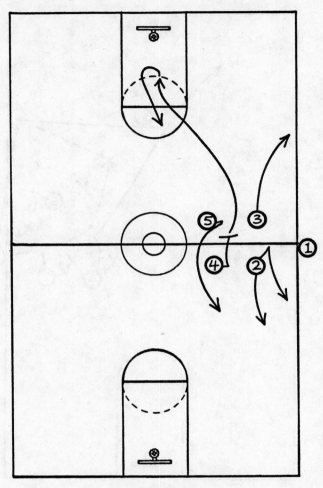

Figure 8-17

in the front court. The other players are in the same places
they took in the first play (Figure 8-18).

On 1's signal 5 breaks to the sideline as 3 and 2
double-screen for 1. Player 3 should fake his move in the
other mid-court play before screening, and 2 should delay

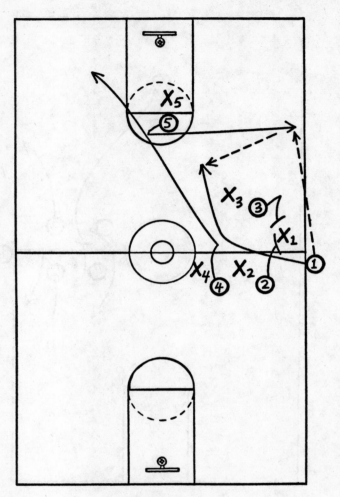

Figure 8-18

his screen until 1 releases the ball. After passing to 5, 1 cuts around the double screen set on his man and sprints to the basket, looking for a pass from 5. Player 5, on receiving the in-bounds pass, may find he can drive to the basket if his defensive man has overcommitted in attempting to pressure the in-bound pass. If he doesn't drive, he looks for 1 sprinting and then to 3 or 2.

Players 3 and 2 must watch for their men switching to pick up 1 when he is sprung free. If X2 picks up 1, 1 should veer away from the ball to open the court for 2, who now becomes the sprinter. Likewise, a switch by X3 to guard 1 means 3 becomes the sprinter.

Player 5 has a scoring option if his defensive man overplays him at the start of the play. If X5 fronts 5 or gets out of position in defensing the anticipated in-bounds pass from 1, 5 may fake going to the sideline and roll to the hoop, signaling for a high pass from 1. If 1 elects not to throw the pass, the other players must break free so he has another passing option before five seconds elapse.

JUMP BALL AT CENTER COURT

A balanced jump ball line-up with a safety tip to the rear to either guard starts the Jug action. The ball is brought up the middle by the guard (1) as the other guard (2) cuts across ahead of him (Figure 8-19). As an alternative, 1 may pass to 2 as shown. Forward 3 on the ball-side goes to the basket area to block for the other forward (4), who goes around the block to receive a possible pass from 2. The jumper (5) goes to the rebounding area on the off side of the hoop. The team is in its Jug offense just moments after the ball has been tipped.

A tip forward (Figure 8-20) sends the nonreceiving side forward (4) streaking to the basket looking for a pass from 3. Player 3 has the following options: (1) hit the off-side guard (2), who is cutting to the basket; (2) give the ball to 1 as he cuts by on his side; or (3) dribble to the basket himself. If he does dribble, or give it to 1, and no shot occurs, 3 continues across the lane around 4's block. The

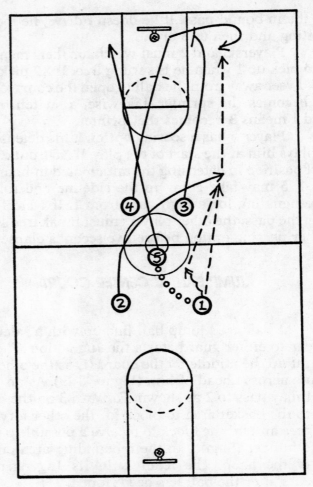

Figure 8-19

jumper (5) assumes off-side rebound responsibilities, and the Jug is going full tilt.

A ball tipped to the side other than the one diagrammed, of course, predetermines that side as the one used for the block, and assignments are changed accordingly.

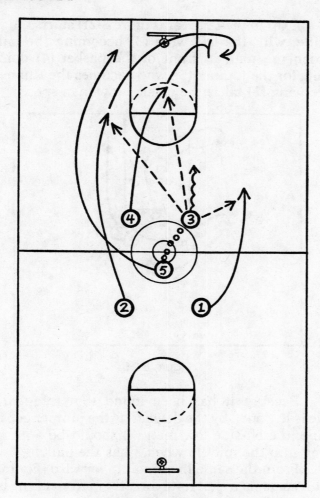

Figure 8-20

JUMP BALL IN THE FRONT COURT

From a defensive diamond set, the ball is tipped back to either rear quadrant. To aid the safety man in anticipating where the ball will go, a signal is made by the jumper prior to the toss-up.

A tip to the left rear (Figure 8-21) starts the Jug on that side, with the left wing (3) becoming the ball-side Shoulder, the man in front of the basket (4) doing the blocking for the jumper (5), who becomes the Runner. The off-side wing (2) takes the off-side low-man spot.

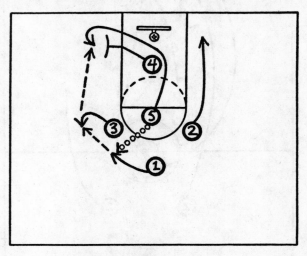

Figure 8-21

Because it has been found that frequently the middle is left open by the defense as the jumper goes out of the lane, the off-side low man (2) should be anticipating flashing into the middle when 3 has the ball.

From the same line-up a tip forward (Figure 8-22) hopefully sets up a shot for 4 directly in front of the basket. Player 4 might pass or make a second tip to either 2 or 3, cutting to the hoop. If no shot is made, or if a shot misses and 2 or 3 captures the rebound but can't shoot, or if 2 or 3 has the ball by virtue of a pass from 4 and can't shoot, the Jug swings into action with a pass out to the jumper (5), who moves out wide on the ball side. He relays the ball to 1, who dribbles (if necessary) to his left and hits 4, who is now a Shoulder. Player 2 runs around the block set by 3.

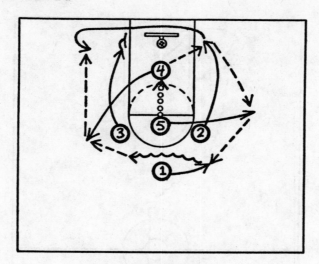

Figure 8-22

TEN—A LAST SECOND SHOT

It's called "Ten" because it can be used within the last ten seconds of a period after gaining possession of the ball in the back court. No matter whether the ball is obtained from a rebound, a steal, a violation, or a made shot, it is given to the Cork as quickly as possible, and it is his job to dribble rapidly up court.

The rest of the team must move as fast as possible to set up a Jug or a partial Jug for him. Frequently one player (usually the one who gives the ball to the Cork) can't get up court ahead of the ball, so he becomes a trailer to the play. Regardless of the number of players arriving in the front court ahead of the ball, the first two set up as a Shoulder and Baseliner, stacked on each other (Figure 8-23). The third player up court takes his normal spot on the Shoulder or Baseliner spot on the side opposite the stack.

On crossing the middle of the court, the Cork may veer toward the stack, in which case the Base on the

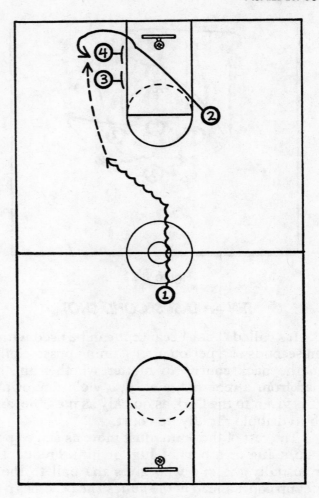

Figure 8-23

nonstacked side (or the Shoulder, if he is the only player on that side) sprints around the double screen of the stack, looking for the ball from the Cork and the subsequent baseline shot. The stacked players must remember to rebound the shot as there may be time for a tip-in of a missed shot.

If the Cork sees a Shoulder on the unstacked side of the Jug or partial Jug, he may veer to that side, using the Shoulder as a screen, and then take a shot. In true Jug fashion the low man on the stack, the Baseliner, should come across the lane and go around a block by the other Baseliner if he is there. If the Cork doesn't shoot, he may feed the baseline Runner or look for the trailer coming up court. At any rate there has been a plan to get a last-second shot, and it has been done in a way not unlike the method of offense used in Jugging.

SINKER—ANOTHER LAST-SECOND SHOT

This play, which is used to obtain a shot in the closing seconds of a period, is run from the Bean Pot. It is keyed by a pass from the Cork to a Shoulder (Figure 8-24), with the Cork going through to the spot vacated by the Baseliner on the ball side. The Baseliner leaves as soon as

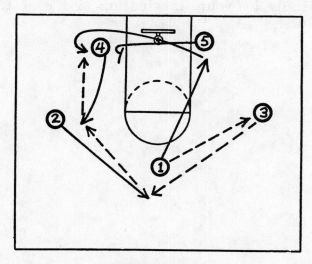

Figure 8-24

he sees the Cork heading at him. The Cork always looks for a return pass as he goes through, although he seldom is open. Player 5 crosses the lane, going away from the ball. The other Baseliner (4) replaces the off-side Shoulder (2), who has filled the Cork spot on top.

The Shoulder with the ball reverses it by passing out to the new Cork, (2), who relays it to the Shoulder (4) on the off-side. Meanwhile the original Cork (1) crosses the lane as a baseline Runner and goes around 5's block to receive a pass from 4.

All nonshooters should crash the boards for the possible tip-in. This is not shown in the diagram. There should be no fear that the opponents will be able to take a shot in the minimal time left in the period; however, if this play is run during any part of a quarter other than the very end, it is important that a normal transitional defensive balance be maintained.

Other auxiliaries can be devised, or existing ones can be modified to fit a Jug pattern or to progress into a Jug pattern after the initial play is completed. You are limited only by your imagination and your team's capabilities.

9

JUGGING IN GAME SITUATIONS

One of the most difficult things coaches have to do is set up gamelike situations in practices. There are countless methods, techniques, gadgets, and ploys to teach skills and concepts, but by far the toughest task is to duplicate the game situation on the practice court.

Bringing a band, cheerleaders, recorded game noises, and token crowds into the gym during practice sessions, as well as dressing the team in game uniforms for intrasquad and intersquad scrimmages may help; but taking the court at game time is such a novel experience for the player that we can't prepare him for everything that affects him in the _real_ game.

In early-season games especially, in spite of hours of having practiced and having been coached, the player is seldom completely prepared for the game. If you recognize this, you can approach the coaching between games with a positive attitude and anticipate the continued improvement of the team.

A Jugging team is not going to run its offense perfectly in the first games of a season, particularly if the Jug is a new offense. You are going to have to allow for

153

continued learning during and between games through the game experience and through practice. During a game, not only should you coach to win, but you should also continue to teach basketball to your players.

To help players during a game you have to communicate with them, and they have to communicate with each other. Hopefully, methods of communication have been established during practice time. Some of the different ways of signaling and communicating verbally have been covered in this book. Regardless of the techniques used, it is essential that the signals, keys, and words used are not too complicated and are understood by all. What may work perfectly in practice may suffer in an actual contest, where outside factors are strong influences.

If you diagram in pregame meetings, at time-outs, at half-time, and at the bench during game time to the substitutes, it is important that the players know how to read your diagrams. They should be exposed to them prior to the start of the playing season. You should have put chalk into your chalk talks in practice sessions so that putting over an idea by diagram during a game is not a new or game-only technique. Game time is not the time for a player to have to figure out new methods.

Because the Cork is the player usually designated to run the offense, he should be trained to remain in contact with you during the game. He needs to be conscious of directions coming from the bench throughout the game. He can check while dropping back on defense, at lulls during play, such as the time immediately after a whistle for a foul, violation, or jump-ball, and even while bringing the ball up court. So that information is understood, and because time is of the essence, it is important that words, numbers, and signals used have clear meaning.

You must be sure that all starters know exactly where they are going to play in the Jug set, which flower if any, is to be used, and anything else you feel is essential information at the start of the game. The important things we know about our opponent, even though covered in practice, bear repetition. The game plan should be spelled out. Nonstarters should understand everything covered for the starters, and they should pay special attention to any specifics that apply to the respective spots they may fill during the game.

Assuming that practically all that is covered in the pregame meeting has been gone over before, you still should review assignments in order for them to be fresh in players' minds. Do the Shoulders and Baseliners know which side of the Jug they will cover in the initial set? Are there specific things they should know about the opponents in relation to exploiting certain aspects of the Jug offense? Is there to be more than one Cork designated? Does everyone know his assignment against the half-court trap? Are there any questions?

During the game, and primarily at the start, you must look for ways to aid your players. The Cork–Shoulder action should be analyzed immediately. Is the pass getting through easily? Do changes have to be made to get the lead pass through? Should any players trade spots? Should the offense be varied? Is a change of personnel warranted, based on situations such as a mismatch, a defensive weakness or strength, the brand of officiating, an off-game by a starter? How is the defense adjusting to the baseline Runner going around the block, to the reverse action, to the Pick-Roll, to the double block? Are we holding our own on the boards? Is a time-out needed to change the offense? Are you communicating with your team leader? Are you giving the bench players information that may help them when they enter the game?

Just as game situations are set up for players in practice, the following scenario attempts to duplicate some aspects of coaching the Jug during the game. All cases presented here have occurred in actual games played by teams using the Jug. No attempt has been made to

incorporate all phases of game coaching. The emphasis is
on the use of the Jug in game situations.

For our hypothetical game we have a brief scouting report on the next opponent. This is presented to our
team in practice sessions, incorporated with the intended
game plan. In their past three games our opponents have
used both a man-for-man and a 2-1-2 zone defense. They
fast-break when it is possible, using their two big men as
key rebounders. These big men use long outlet passes to a
floating guard to start the break. In height they are about
even with us. Their guards are quick, and they hustle on
defense. The two big front-liners are slow but rebound
well.

Using the information available, we emphasize
certain things in pregame practices. In the transition
game, after we lose the ball, we pressure the outlet pass by
the rebounder. The Cork plays a strong safety spot, only
moving up to pick off an outlet pass. Because their guards
are quick, our Cork and Shoulders spend more time on
ball handling and movement skills. We also spend time on
our fast break, hoping to take advantage of their big, slow
men. Along with the work on the break, time is spent on
the secondary action, incorporating Jug principles.

On game day, in our pregame meeting we cover
the entire game plan, including the designation of specific
spots to each starter in the Jug. We remind the team that
we want to take advantage of our Jug strengths and the
opponent's defensive weaknesses. A quick diagramming of
the fast break secondary action is made in order to
emphasize that phase of our game because we will use it
regardless of whether we face man-for-man or zone.

We plan to start two of our regular guards, both of
whom have handled the Cork spot. We want to match the
speed of the opponent's guards and also spread the Cork
responsibilities between the two players who will probably be hustled by the two quick defenders in the front line
of the opponent's 2-1-2 zone. Both Corks are reminded of

their defensive responsibilities once the ball is lost. The other starters are told again about their rebounding responsibilities and their roles in stopping the outlet pass, which kicks off the fast break. The Shoulders are cautioned to be "alive" and help if the Cork is two-timed. The team is asked if there are any questions. If there are any, they are answered.

During the pregame warm-up every player will have a chance to take a few Jug shots at the Shoulder and along the baseline. Before the start of the game the scorebook is checked and, for the purposes of the scenario, it is found that one of their quick guards is not starting. Shall we shuffle our line-up or go with it and watch to see if we will be at a disadvantage with our two small men in our line-up? We decide to stay with the original starters. The opponents are observed during their warm-up. The actions of the big men confirm the scouting report. They are slow. The new man in the line-up is tall, and quicker than the two big men. Will they fast-break? We believe so.

Before the end of the warm-up period we have talked to the nonstarter who would have been one of the Shoulders had we not elected to start with two guards. He will sit next to the coaches at the start of the game in case a quick change in the line-up is needed.

At the jump ball we gain possession, and the team sets up in the Jug. The opponents are matched up defensively with us. Are they in a zone or man-for-manning? The Cork calls for the Dislocate to test the defense, and the dislocating Shoulder is not followed across and around the block. It's a zone. The continuity of Jugging continues until a shot is taken.

Coming up court the next time on offense, the Cork does not announce a zone to his team. Instead he shouts, "Jug." We believe the calling out of the offense to be used is a more positive way of playing basketball, designating what we will do and not what we "think" the opponent is doing. At times a Cork might err in his judgment of what defense we are facing. Letting the opponents know he has made this mistake gives them a lift. Opponents do not need such a gift, ever.

Dislocate is run the first two times up court. The bigger of the two Shoulders dislocates and misses baseline shots. In each case the opponents capture the rebound and kick the ball out to start their break. We tell the Cork to send the shorter Shoulder (the other guard) through if the Dislocate is run again so that we can get more size in our rebounding effort. The bigger Shoulder will be in the middle of our rebound triangle.

The next problem concerns the Cork's difficulty in hitting a Shoulder with his lead pass. The opponent's top man in the 1-2-2 zone, the surprise starter, is much taller than our Cork. It's time to substitute, and the player sitting next to the coaches goes in at the Shoulder, in hopes that the additional height there will help the Cork to get the ball to him. It doesn't seem to make much difference; the Cork is still having problems passing to a Shoulder. A switch is attempted, with the players at the Cork and one of the Shoulder spots trading positions. The offense starts a bit more easily because of the elimination of the mismatch at the Cork spot.

Having an assistant on the bench helps. He has been observing the defensive shifts made against the Jug's baseline run. The two big defenders underneath don't want to wander out of the free throw lane. When the ball goes down to the Runner from the Shoulder, the wing (who was guarding the ball at the Shoulder) follows the ball to the Runner. For a moment, before the defensive point drops back, the Shoulder is left open. If the team does not pick up on this, the Cork is told about it at the first opportunity. "Low triangle," the coach tells the Cork. The Cork should get the word to his teammates so they can play three-on-two basketball, with the Shoulder, the Blocker, and the Runner moving the ball quickly in order to get a shot before the zone shifts to balance things.

In the situation described above, several options are open. The Runner, if he doesn't get a shot, may return the ball immediately to the Shoulder (3 in Figure 9-1), who has stepped toward the basket. The Runner (4) may dump the ball in to the Blocker (5), who is posting. If 5 can't shoot, he may scoop the ball to 3, who is going to the hoop. If the other big defender (X4) comes out to guard 3, 3 may drop the ball off to the other Shoulder (2), who has made his normal Jug adjustment of going to the baseline. A third possibility is for 3, who has received the Cork's pass (Figure 9-2), to feed 5 and then step toward the hoop. If this freezes the wing defender (X3) on him, it means that the 4 is left unguarded, and 5 should give him the ball for an uncontested shot.

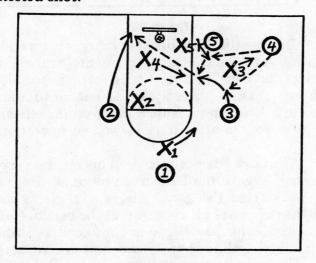

Figure 9-1

If the team does not pick up on these options, diagrams are shown during the first time-out. Another way to get the word out on the court is to explain the set-up to a substitute and have him enter the game with the information about taking advantage of the shift of the 1-2-2 zone.

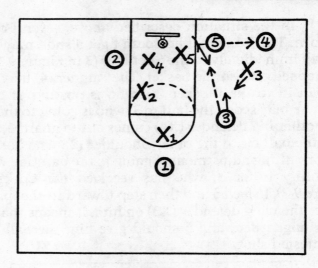

Figure 9-2

During the first quarter other observations are made, and in due course adjustments are made. The Shoulders and Baseliners have been setting up in the same spots every trip up court, so word is sent out to trade sides of the court. A judgment is then made on the effectiveness of the new set-up, after it is viewed in operation for a while.

The Cork has not mixed up his offense very much so far, staying with the Dislocate version of the Jug with which we started the game. He is advised to vary the offense during one of his check-ins at the bench. Next time up he calls T, and the defense is flat-footed as a Shoulder gets an easy baseline shot. In the next offense series the normal Jug movement produces a good shot for the Runner, who for the first time in the game is a Baseliner and not a dislocating Shoulder. As the offense continues, the defensive shifts against the Baseliner coming around the block are evaluated. Are our players taking advantage of miscues by the defense slowness in shifting, overshifting, packing in too tight, and overextension?

As count-down time in the first quarter approaches, the Cork, who has been trained to check the clock, calls for the delay game. This expands the Jug almost out into the Carboy set, and the normal continuity is run without a shot being taken. Our objective is to "eat up the clock" until a designated amount of time is left in the quarter, at which time a last-shot attempt will be made.

If the Cork is facing the clock, he usually needs little help in determining how much time is left in the quarter. If the clock is located behind him at the other end of the court he depends on the Shoulders to keep him informed, especially during the last 15 seconds of the period. With 10 seconds remaining the Cork calls for the ball and, with about 7 seconds left, signals Curl by touching the hair on his head. The Shoulders Curl down and pick for the two Baseliners, who flare out, looking for the pass from the Cork. The pass goes, and there is still time for a possible tip-in after a Baseliner releases his shot. The quarter ends with the opponent denied one last opportunity to score, whether or not we were able to score ourselves.

The seating arrangement at the bench during the quarter break is the same as that used during time-outs. The players coming in from the court sit in the seats vacated by the players who were on the bench. We like the warm Cork (the one who has just been playing) to sit in the center facing the coach, with two warm players sitting on each side of him. The other players will fill the perimeter between the coach and the outside players on the bench.

With a slight lead now going into the second quarter, we plan to be more deliberate, working harder for the closer shots and hitting the boards harder in order to get that second chance to score if the first shot misses. The players are reminded to try to activate the fast break, but to take only high-percentage shots.

Shortly after the start of the second quarter, one of our Baseliners picks up his third foul, so a substitute is sent in for him. The new line-up is now observed as they play.

Because of our more deliberate Jug style, the defense is forced to play more aggressively and has to come out tighter on us. This helps when we run our sideline out-of-bounds plays, which, up until now, have been unproductive because the zone has sagged back.

During this first half of play, whenever we have the ball out of bounds on our baseline, we have run Series A (see Chapter 8), which is standard procedure the first half of all our early-season games. In this way, no signal has to be given or received, and all players know exactly what series will be run.

Close to the end of the second quarter our opponents have possession of the ball and make a field goal with eight seconds left in the period. Our closest player to the ball, as it goes through the net, grabs it and in-bounds to the Cork, who streaks up court. Meanwhile the other players have gone up court to set up in Ten (see Chapter 8), and again we have the opportunity to score by virtue of a plan that fits in with the Jug offense that we have been using throughout the game.

During the half-time break the plan for the second half is covered. We plan to open with the Bean Pot, thus giving the Jug a new look. If the defense stays in their 1-2-2 zone, we should look for the possibility of the Cork penetrating and the Baseliners flashing to the ball.

The Baseliner, who has been charged with three fouls, is told he will start the second half. Along with him at the other Baseliner spot will be the player who had substituted for him in the second quarter. He has done a good job and deserves another opportunity to play. We are curious at this stage of the season about the performance and capabilities of different combinations in the back line.

The two guards who started the game will be back in, one at Cork and the other at a Shoulder spot. It is felt that the guard-Cork will have an easier time passing from the Bean Pot set and that his quickness over the man who had defensed him in the first quarter may allow him to penetrate into the middle of the Pot. By alternating the two guards in the line-up at the Cork spot, we may also tire the top defender in the 1-2-2.

We will continue to fast-break, trying to beat the zone back, and to make their big men run. The team is reminded that they should be ready to adjust if the defense changes against us, and to follow the lead of the Cork.

For the third time in the game at the center jump we use a safety-tip backwards and go directly into the auxiliary play (see Chapter 8). No shot is obtained, so the Jugsters open up into the Bean Pot, and we are "in business."

Instead of facing a 1-2-2, we find a 1-3-1 set-up against us, which shuts off the middle. We hope the Cork realizes this and doesn't try to force his way in as he would against the 1-2-2. We also want the Baseliners to look for the opportunity to flash into the seam between the zone's wings and their middle men.

The Cork-to-Shoulder pass starts the offense with the ball-side Baseliner blocking the one defender under the basket while the other Baseliner runs around his block. The change in the opponent's defense has not stopped the running of the Jug. Yet we wonder if the team knows they are now facing a 1-3-1. It is not really imperative at this time that they do know as long as they can run the Jug offense from the Bean Pot set. So far, so good!

Without an order to change coming from the bench, the Cork plans to continue to run the Bean Pot on subsequent trips up court. However, on his next trip up court with the ball, he runs into a half-court trap sprung out of the 1-3-1, and we lose the ball. Immediately the word is out that the Carboy is on. The coaches are calling it, and the Cork relays the word to the team. It is repeated again to all during a line-up for a free throw soon after.

The Carboy is effective, and the opponents abandon their trap. They go back into a 1-2-2 zone, which they used in the first half. Against the Bean Pot they are spread out, and the Cork does some free-lancing into the middle, taking advantage of the space there. A bit later in the quarter the other guard takes over at Cork and tries his skill at penetrating.

Midway in the quarter our bigger Baseliner picks up his fourth foul and is taken out of the game. The other Baseliner, who started the game, goes in for him, and soon he is whistled down for his second and third fouls while attempting to rebound with the opponent's biggest and best rebounder. A change is needed, so the Baseliner with three fouls switches spots with a Shoulder (not the guard Shoulder). We go back to the normal Jug set in hopes that the mismatch in size at one Shoulder spot will give us some shots there, and that the mismatch underneath, which benefits the opponent, will not be much different than it would have been if we had left in the player with four fouls, who, in fear of being charged with a fifth foul, certainly would not have been able to rebound aggressively.

One height advantage now held by the opponents makes it possible for them to operate better at their end of the court, and our lead rapidly diminishes. A time-out is called, during which we decide to nurse our slight lead for the balance of the quarter while one of our big men is on the bench and the other one has three fouls.

Anxiety to get the ball forces the opponents to foul, and presently one of their big men is in foul trouble and goes to the bench with four. Things are evening up. The quarter ends with a last-second shot obtained from the Shoulder Flex (Figure 3-2 in Chapter 3) when the Blocker comes up the lane opened by the flexing Shoulder, receives the ball from the Cork, and takes his turn-around shot.

With only a slim lead, we decide to start the fourth quarter off in a more aggressive fashion. The original starting five is in, and on the jump ball we tip forward instead of back (as we have done three times before). The opponents have conceded us the tap, and in their attempt to steal a tip back as expected, they aid us in our play, which has a guard streaking to our basket.

Their man with four fouls is matched up with our four-foul man, so the Cork is told to work the Jug on their side of the court in an attempt to give the ball to our man posting low. We score twice using this tactic before their big man fouls out in his determination to prevent a third attempt. A baseline out-of-bounds play in which we run Series D for the first time in the game catches our opponents unaware (we had been running Series A up to this point) and ups our lead by another two points—and we don't relinquish it for the balance of the game.

In the latter part of the game some time-outs are used to cover some important points with the team. We try to stress to the players not to be automatons, to work harder on taking advantage of defensive lapses, and not to be so predictable in their moves. We put in a rule that we will not go into the reverse action until we come back to the strong side after the ball is cleared out to the Cork.

Because one of our guards is a good baseline shooter and because we want him to develop confidence in his shot in special situations, we call for Cork Through (Figure 3-4 in Chapter 3) to finish the game. Since two Corks have been alternating at that spot, there is a mix-up, and the wrong Cork (not the good baseline shooter) handles the ball and runs the play. He makes the shot; the crowd screams; and the coach appears to be a mastermind. Only the team and the assistant coach know of the error, but in the glow of victory they don't reveal it and go along with the coach in accepting the accolades.

Our post-mortems are held on the next practice day, at which time we cover the good and bad aspects of our game. In discussing the offense we remind the team of the things they did that worked, and we discuss why they worked. If we earned a good shot and took it while Jugging, that is good, whether or not the shot is successful. This is stressed, so that failure to connect on a shot doesn't negate good offensive work. The reason for some things not working is discussed. Because it is early in the season, a lot of attention is given to how the team adjusted to the changes in defense that the opponent threw at them and how the Jug handled all of them. Very little time, if any, is given to the coaching error of not specifying which player should have taken the last shot of the game. If it is discussed, it's in the light of explanation that the coach, too, is only human.

10

_____JUG
DRILLS_____

Specific skills used in Jugging may be perfected by incorporating them into drills used to teach most of the offensive fundamentals of basketball. Likewise, special drills designed to include primarily Jug skills can be used to teach many other basic skills needed in the sport.

The majority of drills presented here have been derived from a breakdown of Jug action. They have all been tried, reevaluated on a seasonal basis, and modified. You may want to devise drills that will fit in with your own style of coaching and your philosophy of running a practice.

THE CORK–SHOULDER TRIANGLE

Because the Cork-to-Shoulder pass is such an important element of the Jug and the key to the start of the offense, much time should be spent on this part of it. Drills involving the players who will be making these passes—conceivably all of your team—should be used. You should attempt to have players practice in the spots they will occupy in games. With a Cork and two Shoulders set up on the court in normal Jug spots, the following drills are conducted:

1. Basic Passing Drill: The three players exchange passes, with the Shoulder always returning the Cork's pass to the Cork. The Cork may pass to either Shoulder. All use the two-hand-overhead, two-hand-bounce, one-hand-bounce, cross-over-one-hand, cross-over-two-hand, and chest passes.

2. Two on Two: Two defenders are added to Drill 1. When the defense is on each Shoulder, the Cork must stay in place. The Shoulders may move about in the Shoulder area, freeing themselves to receive the pass from the Cork. When the Cork and one Shoulder are defensed, the Cork may dribble, may use a Shoulder's screen, and may switch spots with a Shoulder in an effort to make his pass or receive the ball.

3. Three on Three: With the defense matched up with the passers, the Shoulders are allowed to go to the basket to receive the Cork's pass whenever the defense overplays them, thus keeping the defense honest in their attempts to stop the Cork–Shoulder pass. A variation of this drill is to have the defense trap the Shoulder who receives the Cork's pass. Have the defensive man guarding the Cork follow the ball and double on the Shoulder. The trapped Shoulder does not have to abide by the rule that allows him to pass only to the Cork; he may, in this case, pass to the other Shoulder. A third modification of the drill is to put two defenders out on the Cork while the third defensive man zones in between the Shoulder in a 2-1-2 zone fashion.

4. Three on Four: The defense is set with a point man out on the Cork, and the other three men are placed across the middle of the court as they would be in a 1-3-1 zone line-up. The wings will play in a variety of spots in relation to the Shoulders, including being in front, inside of them, to the outside, and behind them. The middle man clogs the area between the Shoulders. Another defensive set may be used, a 2-2 formation with two men harassing the Cork and the other two guarding the Shoulders. This is not the usual formation the offensive triangle would face under game conditions, but the drill can be a confidence builder when the three Jugsters do complete their passes. From either the 1-3 or 2-2, traps may be sprung on the Shoulder receiving the ball. The triangle is forced to be very active in this drill if it is to succeed.

5. *Facing the Basket:* There is no single rule for the stance of the Shoulders in receiving the Cork's pass. The position of the Shoulder as he catches the ball depends largely on the actions of the defense. During the triangle drills work is done on coaching the Shoulder to position the defensive man near him by use of hips, arms, and wide stance to hold off the defender. In the Facing-the-Basket Drill, at first the Shoulders are guarded from behind by two defenders. The Shoulder meets the pass from the Cork, plants both feet, and after catching, turns to the outside with an outside-foot pivot. Facing the basket, he is allowed five seconds to get off a shot over the defense, drive by the defense or, as a last resort, pass back to the Cork.

The same drill may be used with the defense playing on the inside of the Shoulders. The Shoulders attempt to meet the ball as in the other drill, but usually the pass goes to the outside hand if the defense is pressuring on the inside. The inside foot of the Shoulder is usually advanced. In this position, as the ball is caught, a drop step by the outside foot or a pivot to the outside is possible, followed by a quick jump shot or a drive to the hoop as options. Again the five-second limitation is placed on the Shoulder when he catches the ball.

After these drills have been used, add another option for the Shoulder with the ball: a pass to the off-side Shoulder, who drops to the baseline as he would in the Jug offense when the Cork–Shoulder pass has been completed.

THE SHOULDER–BASE TRIANGLE

This is the second phase of the basic Jug pattern. The Shoulder has received the ball and is facing the basket. The passes used are the same as those practiced in the Cork–Shoulders Triangle drills. In the drills where there is defense, the man being defensed should read the defense and react accordingly; for example, a defender who goes around the block on the baseline side to cover the Runner should be "scorched" by the Runner ducking back and coming out in front of the basket to receive the pass from the Shoulder.

In the following four drills the offensive players should limit their activity, after the baseline run, to only one side of the court. The offensive players should rotate from Shoulder to far Baseliner to near Baseliner to Shoulder after each turn and then switch to the other side of the court to run the same drill three more times with the same player progression.

1. Baseliner Run: The Baseliners are in position, and one Shoulder has the ball. When the Shoulder slaps the ball, the near Baseliner turns inward to block, and the far Baseliner runs the baseline around the block to receive the ball from the Shoulder. The blocking Baseliner pivots back to face the ball and to receive a pass from the Runner. The Baseliner may pass either to the Shoulder or back to the Runner. Passing continues in any order desired for a specific time, or a specific number of passes could be designated before starting over with the three players in new spots.

2. *Three on One:* This drill (Figure 10-1) has the same passing as Drill 1. One defensive man is added, and he starts in a position midway between the original spots of the two Baseliners. He allows himself to be blocked on the first baseline run and continues guarding the Blocker when he becomes a low post. On the second run, with the offensive players starting in the same spots, he goes around the block and guards the Runner. On the third run, he picks up the Shoulder after being blocked. Finish the drill with the offensive players at their original spots, with the Runner, Blocker, and Shoulder doing the shooting. After each shot, all four players rebound.

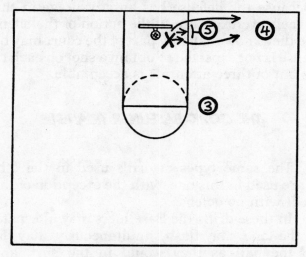

Figure 10-1

The progression in this drill should include the defensive man, who gets into the rotation between the far Baseliner and the near one.

3. *Three on Two:* Start with the defense on the two Baseliners. The defender on the near Baseliner fights around the block to guard the Runner. If possible, the Runner shoots, and all rebound. If he can't shoot, the

passing drill continues, during which the Runner's defensive man drops in on the Baseliner when the ball goes to him. Only the Baseliner and Runner may shoot. Another version of the same drill is to shift one defensive man to guard the Shoulder and have the other man guard the two Baseliners alternately. Add to the drill by having the defensive man on the passer follow the ball to the receiver whenever he is guarded by the other defensive man.

4. Three on Three: Two defenders are in the back line, and one is up guarding the Shoulder. The defense is zoning, moving with the ball and attempting to stop the play. Because the defense has an advantage in this drill due to their overexposure to the action of the offense and because they know that only part of the court may be used, the offense is not expected to obtain a shot on each try. One success out of three attempts is acceptable.

THE CORK–BASELINER TRIANGLE

The same types of drills used in the other triangles are used in this one, with the exception of the basic pass drill with no defense.

In these drills the Baseliners may alternate flashing up the lane, may flash simultaneously, may flare out and to the ball as they would in the curl, and may alternate flashing to a high post. At the high post, they turn and look for the other Base crossing in front of the basket.

THE PICK-ROLL DRILLS

1. Three on One: Three Jugsters are used: one at an extended Shoulder position with the ball (Figure 10-2),

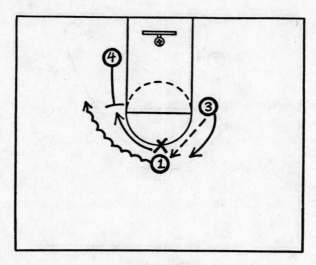

Figure 10-2

another at the Cork spot, and a third at the Baseliner rebound spot, which is away from the ball. One defender is on the Cork, and he varies his defense by allowing the pass, denying it, and overplaying it. The Cork must work to get free to receive the pass from the Shoulder (3). He is allowed to back-door his defense if it is overcommitted and to take a shot from the free throw area. When the ball goes out to the Cork, he starts his dribble toward the Baseliner (4), who is coming up to pick for him. The Cork takes a jumper just past the pick. The Baseliner, on contact with the defense, rolls to the hoop to rebound. The Cork and the defensive man are also rebounding. The Shoulder does not rebound; in the normal Jug, he would replace the Cork. Therefore, he rotates to the Cork spot ready for the next part of the drill. The other players in the drill rotate from Cork to Baseliner, to defense, to Shoulder.

2. Three on Two: A defensive man on the Baseliner is added to Drill 1. If this man steps out to stop the Cork on the pick, the Cork passes to the Roller; if he doesn't, the Cork takes his shot. A variation of the drill is to have the

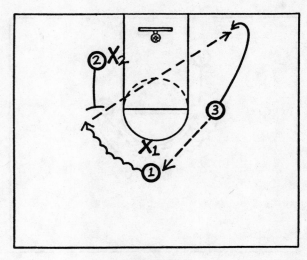

Figure 10-3

Shoulder drop down to the baseline (Figure 10-3) after his pass, taking the spot where the Runner would be in the normal Jug offense. Now the Cork may pass to him before or after the pick occurs—a gamelike situation. It is suggested that this variation not be used early in Jug training because the shift from Shoulder to Runner is not part of the Jug continuity but merely an expedient in the drill to present another situation. When using a Runner in this drill, have him shoot after receiving the pass from the Cork. To avoid confusion in rotating in this drill, rotate just the offensive players until the drill is completed, keeping the same players on defense.

SHOOTING DRILLS

Called "Shooting Drills" because the shot is emphasized, these drills also incorporate movements and situations that occur in the Jug offense, so that practice in aspects other than shooting is included. When the Jug is broken down for shooting, additional practice is obtained in setting the desired continuity of offensive movement.

1. Quick Shoulder Shot: This shot is obtained in games against passive zones, or when there is a height or jumping ability mismatch at the Shoulder spot. The Cork, with the ball, passes to either of the two Shoulders. A defensive man is stationed midway between the Shoulders at the outside of the free throw circle near the basket. As soon as the Shoulder receives the ball he faces the basket and shoots. He must complete the shot in one motion after catching the ball because the defensive man is coming right at him to stop the shot. Both Shoulders and the defense rebound. The Shoulder is not allowed to dribble, and he can return the ball to the Cork only once. More than one return pass allowed would make it possible to wear down the defense so that the point of the drill would be lost. The defensive man must either block the shot or capture the rebound if the shot is missed in order to replace the Shoulder in the drill. The Shoulder rotates to the Cork spot, and the Cork to defense.

2. Runner's Shot: The Runner crosses the lane from his Baseliner spot, goes around the Blocker, and receives the ball from a Shoulder. A defensive man stationed in front of the basket is not allowed to go around the Blocker until the Runner is past the Blocker. The shooter should catch the ball and square up to the basket before shooting. If the defender is coming at him fast, preventing the shot, the Runner may feed the blocker, who is now posting low. The Runner now takes no more than two steps to free himself for a return pass and his consequent shot. Progression is from Shoulder to Runner, to Blocker, to defense, to Shoulder.

The same drill may be used to practice the Shoulder's Dislocate shot by replacing the baseline Runner in the drill with another shoulder, who becomes the Runner.

3. Cork and Shoulder: Players are located at the Shoulder, Runner, and Cork spots on one side of the court, and a defensive man is guarding the Runner, who has the ball. The ball is relayed to the Shoulder, who may shoot or pass it on to the Cork. The Cork may shoot or return the ball to the Shoulder. The defense follows the ball, attempting to stop a shot at the Shoulder and Cork spots. The ball is allowed to go back from Cork to Shoulder only once. The Shoulder, the Runner, and the defense rebound any shot taken. The defense wins if it prevents a shot. Progression is from defense to Cork, to Shoulder, to Runner, to defense.

4. Cork and Roller: At first a defensive man is guarding a Baseliner. The Baseliner comes up to pick for the driving Cork, and the defense steps out to stop the driver. The Baseliner rolls on contact with an imaginary defensive man on the Cork, and the Cork attempts to pass to the Roller for his lay-in. The pass is a scoop, a one-hand bounce, or a jump pass, depending on the position of the defensive man. Later, add defense on the Cork and allow a switch on defense, with the defender (who was screened) staying with the Roller. Another variation gives the defender who is guarding the screener the option of picking up the Cork after the pick or staying with his man, the Baseliner. When there is no switch, the Cork should be ready to take his shot if he has eluded his defensive man. After a certain number of baskets have been made, or if you prefer, after a certain number of tries have been stopped by the defense, have the players trade assignments.

5. Double Screen: Start with the ball in possession of a player at one end of the free-throw line (Figure 10-4). He is the Roller. He passes out to a Cork and rolls around the double screen formed by the Baseliner and the Runner on the other side of the lane. The Runner does not move from his usual spot on the baseline until the Roller makes

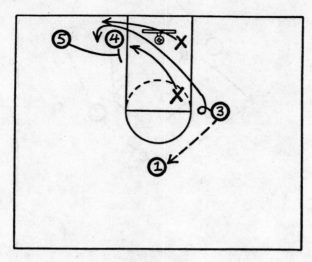

Figure 10-4

his pass to the Cork. A defensive man on the Roller follows him to the basket and then zones in front of the basket.

Another defensive man who has been staying in front of the hoop goes around the double screen to guard the Roller. The Cork hits the Roller if he is open; if not, he fakes a pass and looks for the top man in the screen (former Runner) to roll across the lane in front of the basket—a normal Jug move. The zoner in front of the basket tries to stop him. Meanwhile the low man in the double screen can flash to an opening, so the other defender must try to contain him. In this four-on-two drill the offense should score frequently. If they continually score off the same option, allow the defense to cheat and force the use of another option. Progression is from Cork to Roller, to low man, to high man, to Runner, to Cork.

6. *Squaring the Lane:* This drill (Figure 10-5) is for the Baseliner Blocker's shot in the reverse action when the Pick-Roll is not used. It is also designed for the weak-side Baseliner's shot when the ball is reversed to him. Five

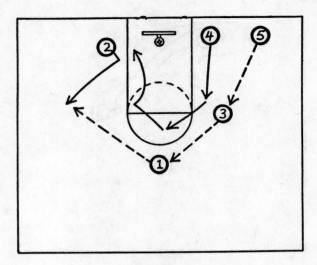

Figure 10-5

offensive players and one defensive player are used. On the strong side, the ball is in the hands of the Runner on the baseline; there is a Blocker and also a man at an extended Shoulder position on that side. The Cork is in position; a Baseliner is in his position on the weak side.

When the pass from Runner (4) to Shoulder (3) is made, the Blocker (5) starts to square the lane by following the ball, looking for a pass from the Shoulder first. If he does not receive the pass, he moves toward 1, who has received the ball from 3. Player 1 passes to 5, or to Baseliner 2, who has come up to receive the Cork's pass as the reverse action moves to the weak side. If the ball goes to 2, 5 cuts to the hoop looking for a pass. A defensive man stays with the Blocker as he squares the lane, and he tries to stop the pass to 5 and the shot if 5 gets the ball. If 5 can't shoot, he passes the ball back to the player who had passed it to him, and the drill continues.

A variation is to allow the weak-side Baseliner (2) to take his shot as the ball is reversed. Player 5 and his defensive man rebound the shot, along with 4 and 3.

After the Blocker's shot, or if he is unable to shoot in his squaring run, the players move up one position, rotating as follows: the Cork goes to Shoulder, to Runner, to Blocker, to defense, to Baseliner on weak side, to Cork.

7. *Low Post:* One player is at the brick, chesting a defensive man, who is in the lane. A Runner is out on the baseline, and a Shoulder is in position on that side of the court. The Shoulder slaps the ball as a signal for the Blocker to pivot and face the ball, and for the defensive man to become active. The drill becomes a 3-on-1 game, with the Shoulder and Runner passing to each other and in to the posting Baseliner. Only the post is allowed to shoot. Progression is from defense to Blocker, to Shoulder, to Runner, to defense.

Another way to run this drill is to specify the type of shot you want the post to take and have the defense apply only token pressure. The post receives the ball from either Runner or Shoulder, and then he passes out to a player other than the passer. Following that pass, the post makes his move, receives a return pass, and works for his shot.

8. *Medium Post:* A Cork, two Shoulders, and a Baseliner are in Bean Pot spots (Figure 10-6). The Cork passes to the Shoulder on the side that has no Baseliner. The Baseliner (5) flashes to the ball, receives it from 2, turns, shoots, and rebounds. He is aided in rebounding by the nonpassing Shoulder (3). Whoever rebounds the ball clears it out to the Cork. As soon as 5 takes a new Baseliner spot, the Cork passes to the other Shoulder (3), and 5 again flashes to the ball, and the drill is repeated. After a shot by the Baseliner from each side, players rotate Baseliner to Shoulder, to Cork, to Shoulder, to Baseliner.

9. *Curl and T:* A Cork, a Shoulder, and a Baseliner on the same side set up with the ball at the Cork. After the

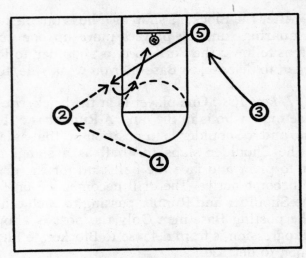

Figure 10-6

Shoulder drops back to his T position, the Cork passes to him for the shot. The Baseliner rebounds and clears the ball out to the Cork. From the same line-up, the Shoulder peels out to his T spot, and the Baseliner flashes up to the free throw line to receive the Cork's pass; the Baseliner turns, shoots, and rebounds with the Shoulder. The ball is cleared out to the Cork, and in the third part of the drill the Shoulder curls down to screen for the Baseliner, who steps out for his shot as he would in the Curl. Rotation is from the Cork to Shoulder, to Baseliner, to Cork.

10. Competitive Shooting: There is an element of competition between offense and defense in some of the above shooting drills, yet more competition may be obtained by using the traditional types of shooting games, in which one part of the team is pitted against another part. Usually a score is kept. Instead of merely using certain spots for shooting, you can use Jug movements and shots obtained in the Jug offense. This procedure will drill the team in certain aspects of the offense, and stress the shots that will occur in games.

FAST BREAK—SECONDARY PHASE

After you have decided how you wish to incorporate Jug action in the secondary phase of your fast break (for example, wing men crossing, keying on the same side as the ball handler, always going to a certain side, using the trailer), you can add it to any fast break drills you run. Limit the shots that result from the break itself, and encourage more attention to the secondary part of it.

1. Three on Two: Set up three lines at mid-court, facing the basket (Figure 10-7). The first players in each line fill three lanes, going against two defenders who are in a tandem formation in front of the basket. The ball is dribbled by the middle man, and the two wing men fill the outside lanes of a simulated fast break shell. The top defender is to stop the dribbler; and the bottom defender, although usually trained to hold and move out to guard whichever wing receives a pass, takes one of the wing men as he cuts to the hoop. The wing man picked up by the defense stops at the brick on his side of the lane, and the other wing comes across the lane around his block to receive the ball from the middle man. If in your fast break one of the wings always crosses the lane to go around the other's block, have him do so in this drill. If your wings key on the side the dribbler takes as he nears the top of the key, use that method in your drill. Rotate from line to line, trading off on defense.

2. Four on Two: If you use a trailer in your secondary action, incorporate him in this drill. This merely adds a fourth line of trailers in Drill 1.

3. Full-Court Continuous Action: A minimum of 12 players is needed to run this traditional fast break drill if you wish to include a trailer in the break. Before you start to work on the secondary phase of the break, it would be a

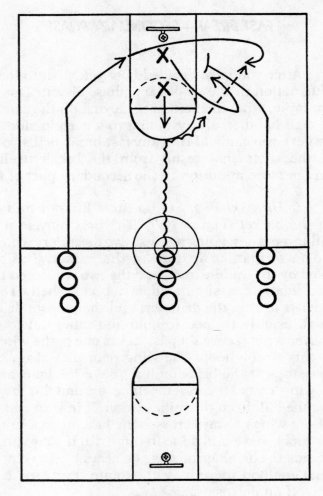

Figure 10-7

good idea to drill your players in the basic fast break
aspect and then add the secondary phase.

The fast break drill is diagrammed in Figure 10-8.
Players 1 through 6 take a turn on defense each time before
joining the offense. They try to stop the break during their
turn on defense and, on obtaining the ball, make an outlet
pass to new offensive players and then fill in the fast break

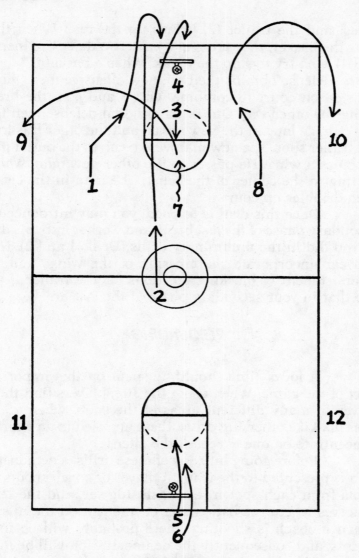

Figure 10-8

lanes. The odd-numbered players beyond 6 always line up on the same side of the court, and the even-numbered players line up on the opposite side of the court.

The break shell is composed of four men; the dribbler (7) is in the middle two wings; 1 and 8 outside lanes; and the trailer (2) brings up the rear. When they near the basket, they are met by the two defensive men (3 and 4), who try to stop the break. When a basket is scored or the defense obtains the ball, new offensive men (9 and 10) step on court to combine with 3 and 4 in the break going the other way. One of the original defense men fills one outside lane in the new break, and the other fills in at the trailer spot. The new man who receives the outlet pass becomes a wing. He passes to the other new man, who is cutting to the center of the court. The man in the center then dribbles up court.

Once this drill is learned, you may introduce the secondary phase of the fast break and work it into this drill as you did in the preliminary drills (Drills 1 and 2). Now you can incorporate the crossing of the wings and the establishment of blocking positions for the trailer if you use that in your secondary phase of the fast break.

REBOUNDING

A lot of time should be spent on this important part of the game. When using the Jug, players find themselves in many different areas of the court when a shot goes up. Like other Jug drills, these are used in an effort to concentrate on one aspect of the offense.

Before going into any of these drills, a demonstration is presented to the team. A player or coach shoots ten shots from each spot in the basic Jug set, and the team observes where the ball comes off the rim on the misses. When a coach is shooting, there probably will be more misses, and consequently the demonstration will be more effective. It is never sound to have a player intentionally miss shots, and if the coach misses a shot during the demonstration, he can always claim that it was intentional for the benefit of the demonstration. Shots are also taken from the Runner's spot, the Cork's spot after the Pick-Roll, and from the low-post spot.

1. Spot Shooting: With five players in the Jug set, the Cork shoots five times, and the other four players rebound offensively, attempting to tip in any misses. A rebound ring inserted in the basket results in more rebounding and serves to inspire better shooting. The same procedure is used at each spot. Each player has a turn at shooting, while all but the Cork rebound. During the drill it is advisable to mention court balance and readiness to go on defense.

Next add two defensive men, placed inside the Baseliners, and repeat the drill with the defensive men attempting to block out the offense and capture the rebound themselves. Stress that *movement* is to offensive rebounding what *position* is to defensive rebounding. *Move* before the shot; *move* while the ball is in the air; and *move* when it hits the rim. The defense should attempt to stop a second shot if the offense gains possession. Finally, add a third defensive rebounder at the center of the free throw line before the shot is taken.

The addition of players, each located at the midcourt hash mark, gives the defense the option of making the outlet pass if it captures the rebound. The Jugsters should try to impede the outlet pass and should retreat on defense when the ball is lost. Allow the new players to advance the ball across the ten-second line, and count how many Jugsters have come back over the line with them.

2. Flow Shots: Continuing the use of a basket insert, have the Jugsters run through the basic Jug action. At the sound of your whistle a shot will be taken by a player. Now, check the rebounders as they seek to tip in missed shots. Add defensive men, one at a time, and continue the drill, using your whistle to trigger a shot. Finally, allow the team that was on defense to bring the ball up court in a fast break. Check the Jugsters' reactions to the transition game, especially the Runner out on the baseline and the Roller behind the double screen. These players have a tendency to become fixtures in these spots when a shot goes up. To save time, the team that ran the fast break sets up in a Jug at the other end of the court and performs the same drill, with the original Jugsters going on defense.

This drill may be run using other Jug sets and Jug action, so that all possible rebound situations are duplicated in the drills.

PREGAME WARM-UPS

You can't count on all opponents zoning, so not all pregame drills have to tie in with the Jug; however, the following drills don't take much time to run, do cover some basic Jug moves and shots, and can be used as warm-ups in conjunction with your other drills.

1. Cork and Two Shoulders: A player is at each Shoulder spot, and there is a line of Corks (Figure 10-9). The first two Corks in line have a basketball. The first Cork passes to the right Shoulder and runs to a spot on the outside of the other Shoulder. The Shoulder who receives the ball faces the hoop, shoots, and follows his shot. He clears the ball out to the third Cork in line. Meanwhile the second Cork, as soon as he sees the shooter regain possession of his ball, passes to the left Shoulder and runs to the right Shoulder spot, which was vacated by the first shooter. The left Shoulder does the same thing as the right Shoulder. After the Shoulders clear the ball, they take a position at the end of the Cork line.

2. Dislocate Move: This drill is similar to Drill 1, except that the Shoulder receiving the Cork's pass does not shoot; he passes to the other Shoulder, who has Dislocated and run around an imaginary block on the ball side. The ball goes to him, and he shoots. All other parts of the drill are the same as in Drill 1.

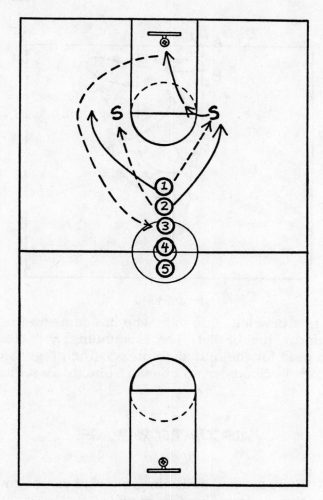

Figure 10-9

3. Baseline Runner: The first two players in the Cork line have a ball (Figure 10-10). Cork 1 passes to the right Shoulder, who passes to the left Baseliner coming around an imaginary block on the right side. The Runner shoots and rebounds along with the Shoulder. The rebounder clears out to the third Cork. Cork 1 has replaced the Shoulder and receives the pass from Cork 2; then he

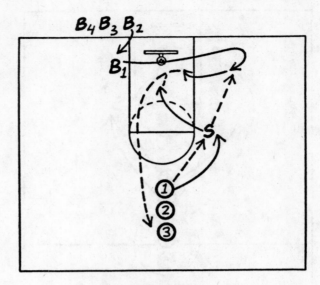

Figure 10-10

passes to a new left Baseliner, who has come on from off court under the basket. The rebounding and clearing pattern used for the first shot follows. The progression is from Cork to Shoulder, to off-court line, to Baseliner, to Cork.

HALF-COURT SCRIMMAGES

There are few limitations on what can be covered in half-court scrimmages. To pinpoint or stress specific parts of the Jug certain restrictions may be placed on the Jugsters or on the defense, and special scoring records may be kept—for example, giving more points for a basket scored in a particular way or by a specific player or from a specific spot.

Using a clock and a score board adds life to these scrimmages and makes them more gamelike. They help in the timing of last-second shot plays, out-of-bounds plays used in the last seconds, and in your control game. Special situations may be created, such as designating one offensive player to be in jeopardy of fouling out (4 fouls), assessing four fouls against a designated defensive player, and mismatching at different spots. The Jugsters should adjust to these situations.

FULL-COURT SCRIMMAGES

The controlled full-court scrimmage may be viewed as the culmination of all Jug drills. In a full-court practice session you are extremely close to a true game, so it is important to include any desired part of the Jug offense in the scrimmage. All auxiliary plays may be tried; the half-court trap can be attacked; the secondary phase of the break can be employed; and recognition of defenses can be used.

Restrictions similar to those used in half-court work may be used in the scrimmages; specific game situations may be developed; and practice of adjustment to the transition from offense to defense is possible. It is suggested that the clock, score board, and officials be utilized, if available, for some of these scrimmages.

SOME LAST WORDS ON DRILLS

Whatever happens on the court during a game is the result of whatever has been happening in your practices. This old coaching adage holds for the use of the Jug. The team that runs a near-perfect Jug during a game doesn't do it by accident; it is due to the skills and capabilities of the athletes and how well they have been trained. It is our job to make sure that practices are learning times.

Drills can be tedious and boring for basketball players. You have to find ways to make them more stimulating, especially as the season progresses. One way to add some zest to drills is to invoke the reward-penalty system. When competition of any kind is added to a drill, it spices it up. Further life and spirit are added by including a reward for the winners, whether it be the privilege of showering first at the end of practice or a soft drink to finish off practice. Whatever you do in this line has to fit into your style and your personal philosophy of dealing with your team. And don't forget the possibility of: "Losers run two suicide line drills; winners, you don't have to run any liners."

INDEX